NASHVILLE BEER

A HEADY HISTORY OF MUSIC CITY BREWING

CHRIS CHAMBERLAIN

AMERICAN PALATE

Published by American Palate
A Division of The History Press
Charleston, SC 29403
www.historypress.net

Front cover: Carol M. Highsmith's America. *Library of Congress, Prints and Photographs Division.*

First published 2014

Manufactured in the United States

ISBN 978.1.62619.539.4

Library of Congress CIP data applied for.

CONTENTS

III. OTHER BREWERY PROJECTS: YESTERDAY, TODAY AND TOMORROW

ACKNOWLEDGEMENTS

While a lot of my friends sarcastically commented about what a tough job it must have been to write a book about so many wonderful Middle Tennessee breweries, it really would have been a difficult task without the cooperation of the members of the local brewing community. You would think that of all the many interviews that I conducted for the book, I would have encountered at least one person who was even mildly unpleasant. That was indeed not the case as the busy entrepreneurs were extremely generous with their time and information, despite the fact that running a brewery is more than a full-time job since every brewery owner has responsibility for production, sales, marketing, distribution and brand evangelism. It is especially gratifying that these people all took the time to answer questions, allow me to poke around their breweries and take pictures and basically bug them until this book almost wrote itself directly from their entertaining anecdotes.

Specifically, I'd like to thank the following people whose voices I have tried to recreate for the readers of this book as they discover the fascinating stories behind the growth of the Middle Tennessee brewing community: Kent Taylor of Blackstone; Karen Lassiter of Boscos; Brad Mortensen and John Burgess of Rock Bottom; Linus Hall and Neil McCormick from Yazoo; Don and Dave Sergio from Calfkiller; Derrick Morse and Chris and Jane Hartland from Cool Springs Brewery; Bailey Spaulding, Robyn Virball and Steven Wright of Jackalope; Mark, David and Andrew Kamp from Turtle Anarchy; Ben Bredesen of Fat Bottom Brewing; Ozzy Nelson of Mayday

Brewery; Ken Rebman from Czann's; Carl Meier and John Owen of Black Abbey; Garr Schwartz and Christian Spears of Tennessee Brew Works; Michael Kwas and Steve Scoville of Little Harpeth; and Scott Swygert of Honky Tonk Company. This book, and the entire craft beer community of Nashville, would be far inferior without your talents.

Others who were instrumental in helping to gather the information and photographs for this project include Heather Davisson, Deb Varallo, Kelsey Griffith, Courtney Sandora, Leah Spivey, Adam Jones, Niki Giacchina, Nelson Eddy and the Jack Daniel's Distillery. Mark Dunkerly, Doc Downs, Austin Ray and Matt Leff were very helpful as resources and are people I always enjoy bending an elbow with. Steve Cavendish and Steve Coomes are two colleagues and friends who offered guidance, and I'll always be grateful for your enthusiasm toward my writing projects. Kirsten Schofield, Chad Rhoad and Darcy Mahan were my editors at The History Press and were wonderful at keeping me on schedule and keeping my prose sharpened. Thanks to Marty Fitzpatrick for my author's photo and to the Sportsman's Grille in the Village for allowing me to enjoy a midday pint for the photo shoot.

Special thanks to Scott Mertie, who literally wrote the book on the history of Nashville brewing in the nineteenth and twentieth centuries with his treatise *Nashville Beer*. Scott's enthusiasm for my project and his contributions of knowledge and material for this book were invaluable, but I will try to put a value on them by buying him beers for the foreseeable future.

Finally, thanks to my dear friends Jim Reams and Lisa Tinsley for always being there to accompany me to a brewery or taproom when I needed to take photographs or nail down a final detail for a chapter. You both kept me from drinking alone.

INTRODUCTION

Long known as "Music City, USA," Nashville, Tennessee, has undergone a bit of a renaissance of late. Nationally lauded as one of the newest "It Cities," following in the footsteps of hip towns like Austin and Portland, Nashville is enjoying a period in the national spotlight. Of course, the music scene is a primary draw for tourists and new residents, but Nashville is also known for a strong creative community, a business-friendly investment environment and a wealthy and youthful population.

These cultural and demographic aspects also make for a healthy base for a thriving food and drink community. Local eating establishments have experienced unprecedented growth over the past decade, and restaurateurs from across the country are rushing to open new dining outposts to take advantage of the hungry and thirsty populace who pack local eateries and bars.

Another element that Nashville has in common with the past boomtowns of Portland and Austin is a strong and growing craft beer culture. The history of brewing in Nashville can essentially be divided into five time periods. Well, you could say six or seven separate epochs if you count the two long periods during Prohibition and from 1954 to 1988, when no beer was commercially produced in the city. But that would be like counting "off" as one of the twenty-three speeds on your new blender.

The first era of Nashville beer production was based in a brewing background of German immigrants who settled in Nashville in the years around the Civil War to help build the large commercial buildings in the

Yazoo Brewing Company and owner Linus Hall have been integral to the development of many craft breweries in Nashville.

growing downtown. During this period, the city developed a taste for Bohemian-style lagers, which led to Nashville becoming one of Anheuser-Busch's top markets for decades. Locally, a transplanted German via Cincinnati dominated production and sales in the form of the Gerst Brewing Company, Nashville's longest-lasting brewing operation, which represents the second and longest epoch of local brewing history.

With only one major brewery in operation within the city limits for the first half of the twentieth century, Nashville remained a commodity beer market until experiencing the third major division in brewing history in the form of a brewpub boom in the last decade of the century. Four new breweries introduced residents to exotic styles of beers that could previously rarely be found on the shelves of their favorite supermarket, and for a decade, these four entrepreneurial undertakings educated the palates of the drinking class.

Another trailblazer kicked off the latest craft beer explosion in 2003 when Linus Hall decided to make the jump from homebrewer to share his signature style from the tanks of a new brewery that he named Yazoo, in honor of the river that runs through his hometown of Vicksburg, Mississippi. Yazoo stands alone as the representative of the fourth major time division in Nashville brewing. As Yazoo grew in production and reputation around the region, many other brewers and investors saw the opportunity to replicate aspects of Hall's model and open new facilities as part of the current and fifth era of Nashville beer history. Today, more than a dozen breweries produce craft beers for consumption in their taprooms and distribution to bars and retail establishments in the Nashville area.

With the rise of all these breweries, the entire craft beer community has risen like a tide lifting all boats. Festivals abound offering opportunities to sample the wares of local, regional and national breweries, and homebrewing continues to grow. Bars, taprooms and growler filling locations have popped up all over town, with particular focus being placed on craft beers as local products displace the international brands on the tap handles and in the hearts of beer lovers.

Adjunct organizations like service providers to the brewing industry, trade organizations and lobbying groups have also seized the chance to improve the business climate for Middle Tennessee breweries. Similar to how Nashville songwriters make "writing dates" to collaborate on songs to pitch to the publishers on Music Row, local breweries exhibit a strong sense of creative collaboration as they share advice, recipes and even ingredients in an effort to ensure that Nashvillians have access to the best beer possible.

For their part, the drinking public seems to have an insatiable thirst for new products and enjoy actively learning more about the people and stories behind the breweries that produce their favorite drafts, bottles and cans. This book is for them.

PART I

NASHVILLE BREWING
IN THE NINETEENTH AND
TWENTIETH CENTURIES

Chapter 1

THE RISE OF NASHVILLE BREWING IN THE NINETEENTH CENTURY

"MINE EYES HAVE SEEN THE GLORY"

In *Nashville Brewing*, author Scott Mertie's excellent survey of the early history of the beer business in Nashville, the local beer expert and memorabilia collector shares an amazing amount of information from his research and personal collections. Probably the preeminent authority on nineteenth-century Nashville breweries, particularly Gerst, Mertie's treatise is a fascinating record of the infancy of the industry, and he is still a sought-after speaker on the subject years after the book's publication. Much of the following history comes from his extensive research.

Nashville was chartered as a city in 1806, but after being designated as the Tennessee state capital in 1843, population growth began to take off. These new residents needed places to live and work, so construction jobs became an attraction for trained craftsmen. Among this new labor force was a considerable influx of German immigrants. In addition to their talents as builders, some of them brought with them an interest in brewing and drinking beer that they had inherited from the Old Country.

During the 1850s, an enclave of Germans settled in a new neighborhood north of the newly constructed Tennessee State Capitol building, and the region quickly became colloquially known as Germantown. In essence, this was the first suburb of Nashville, and the residents of Germantown quickly expanded their horizons past just construction work to open retail stores, butcher shops and other commercial ventures. The population was diverse economically, with workers' shacks interspersed with large brick townhomes built by the more successful merchants.

A few of the transplanted German Nashvillians dominated the early history of Nashville brewing in a constantly changing landscape of brewery ownership where owners and partners changed so frequently that you could use a scorecard to keep track of them. Jacob Stifel built a small brewery on the corner of South High and Mulberry Streets on a site that would eventually become the home of the powerhouse Gerst Brewing Company for more than half a century. If only Stifel had known that one day that location would be just a few yards from a major interstate at the current address of Sixth Avenue South and Mulberry, perhaps he would have held out for the excellent access to distribution paths. Alas, this particular facility would be bought and sold several times over the next three decades before eventually becoming the longest-lasting brewery in Nashville.

Stifel operated the Nashville Brewery by himself for four years until his business enterprise, and just about all commerce in Nashville, was interrupted by the Civil War in 1863. Middle Tennessee was the site of many major battles during the war, and the uncertainty of the political landscape distracted manufacturers and consumers alike from more trivial pursuits like a draft of lager. Another Nashville brewer whose enterprise was interrupted by the Civil War was Malachi McCormack, who had begun to produce beer in 1859. After tensions heated up between the North and the South, McCormack retreated to Louisville, Kentucky, to continue brewing but would come marching home after the cessation of hostilities.

Stifel found an ally in a man named Mr. Pfeiffer, who partnered with him to operate the brewery for thirteen years. The Stifel & Pfeiffer Brewery was quite large for the era, at four stories tall and employing almost twenty workers at its peak. As was typical of lager breweries, the operation was built around massive underground vaults dug thirty feet down and surrounded by a huge icehouse, which contained three hundred tons of ice all year round to cool more than one hundred hogsheads filled with six hundred to one thousand gallons of lager. The cellars were constructed with an ingenious system of separate compartments that could be shut or filled with straw to provide insulation for all that ice, which was a rare commodity in Nashville, especially during long, hot summers. Ventilation through the vaults allowed conditioned air to be passed to the holding tanks and to draw off warmer air.

In 1869, Stifel and Pfeiffer produced five thousand barrels of beer, the vast majority of which was consumed in Nashville. Sometime before 1873, the name of the brewery was changed to the South Nashville Lager Beer Brewery to indicate the location and style of the brewing process.

Another brewery with similar-sized production as Stifel and Pfeiffer was the Spring Water Brewery, located about six miles from downtown along the major route known as Chicken Pike that ran between Murfreesboro and Lebanon. Fred Laitenburger operated Spring Water and traded on his pristine source of water, as opposed to the urban breweries that bragged about the clean waters of the Cumberland River, which runs through downtown Nashville. Spring Water Brewery operated from 1865 to 1875, selling both ales and lagers to retail establishments from a wholesale warehouse location at 41 Broad Street.

City records also indicate that a number of other breweries operated for short periods after the Civil War, including Rock City Brewery, City Brewery, North Nashville Brewery and Nashville Union Brewery. Like many of the other early breweries in town, there was a crossover of ownership between a small group of businessmen, with Laitenburger and two gentlemen named Mankel and Frank appearing on the various licensing documents of multiple breweries. Mankel and Frank had actually started one of the first small brewing facilities on the riverfront in 1859.

Not all of the beer that was consumed in Nashville during the mid-nineteenth century was brewed locally, though. Entrepreneurs like Adam Diehl, George Lord and James E. Hays prospered by shipping beer from other midwestern breweries to downtown distribution facilities for cold storage and distribution of kegged and bottled brew to taverns and saloons around town using horse-drawn beer wagons. Diehl & Lord was a distribution company formed in 1868 that shipped beer, cider and Tennessee spring water in stoneware bottles. Fourteen years later, the duo built a three-story brick building at the corner of present-day Church Street and First Avenue North. From this facility, Diehl & Lord sold and distributed beverages from brewers like Schlitz and Budweiser throughout the South. The company expanded its enterprise to Memphis, where Lord moved and eventually died in 1889. Diehl ran the company in different locations around Nashville until his death in 1925.

James E. Hays also served as a middleman between midwestern breweries and Nashville consumers as an agent for John Hauck Brewing Co. out of Cincinnati and Milwaukee's Pabst Brewery. Hays purchased the Nashville Beer and Bottling Company from Mr. E.O. Ottenville in 1890. Ottenville had been purchasing bulk beer and sodas for repacking and distribution since he had opened his business in 1875. Hays expanded the operation to

store and keep cold up to ten rail cars of beer barrels, which he distributed in kegs and bottles using a team of wagons.

Around this time, the original Stifel brewery sought some stability after changing hands three times since Stifel and Pfeiffer sold it at auction in 1876. J.B. Kuhn was the high bidder in 1876 and ran the operation for two years before selling it to C.A. Maus. The revolving door of the owner's suite of offices continued to turn in 1880 when John Burkett and a Mr. Herschel bought the brewery from Maus. The name of the brewery was changed to Nashville Brewing Company just in time for it to be sold again in 1882, this time to brothers William and Archibald Walker.

The Walker brothers concentrated on lagers and pilsners, which were becoming the rage both regionally and locally during the 1880s. They continued to brew and distribute beer out of Nashville Brewing Company until finally selling out to two gentlemen from Cincinnati, one of whose names would grace the brands brewed there for the next sixty-four years.

Opposite, top: Adam Diehl and George Lord distributed beer from various midwestern breweries and bottles of Nashville spring water from this facility on the corner of Church and Front Streets. *Courtesy of Scott Mertie from the collection of the Nashville Room of the Nashville Public Library.*

Opposite, bottom: The Walker brothers' Nashville Brewing Company would eventually become the site of the William Gerst Brewing Company. *Courtesy of Scott Mertie from the collection of the Tennessee State Library and Archives.*

CHAPTER 2

WILLIAM GERST BREWING COMPANY

"ROLL OUT THE BARREL"

While many various German Americans were instrumental in the rise of the Nashville brewing industry, two in particular would dominate the first half of the twentieth century—one through his reputation and investment, the other through his operation of and dedication to Nashville's most successful brewery.

William H. Gerst was born into a long line of German brewers in Bavaria in 1847. After apprenticing in the family business until age nineteen, Gerst crossed the Atlantic to America in 1866, eventually finding employment at the Christian Moerlein Brewing Company of Cincinnati. Moerlein himself was a Bavarian immigrant born in Truppach in 1818. Laying a trail for Gerst's eventual path, Moerlein came to America in 1841, where he worked as an apprentice brewer and blacksmith. After settling in the "Over-the-Rhine" German neighborhood of Cincinnati, Moerlein opened his eponymous brewery in 1853.

By 1863, the Moerlein brewery was producing more than twenty-six thousand barrels of beer per annum, and Moerlein had earned a reputation as the preeminent brewer of Cincinnati, a town that loved its beer. At its peak, the brewery exported its products as far away as Europe and South America and was recognized as the fifth-largest brewing operation in the United States. Christian Moerlein continued to run the brewery until his death in 1897, and the operation thrived until it was forced to shutter by Prohibition in 1920. The brand was revived by the Hudepohl Brewing Co. in 1981 and continues to operate out of a new facility built in the

Born in Bavaria in 1847, William Gerst came to Nashville via Cincinnati in the 1880s and dominated the local brewing scene for decades. *Courtesy of Scott Mertie from the collection of the Nashville Room of the Nashville Public Library.*

Over-the-Rhine neighborhood in 2013.

As soon as Gerst went to work for Moerlein, he was quickly recognized for his talents as both a brewer and a manager. As a brewmaster, Gerst was entrusted with the production, and as a foreman, he was instrumental in breaking union strikes. In 1888, Gerst earned his master brewer's certificate and was elected the second president of the United States Brewmasters' Association a year later.

So when Moerlein had an eye for expansion, Gerst was a natural partner for the venture. Their acquisition target was the old Nashville Brewing Company that had changed hands so many times during its first thirty years of operation. The two gentlemen purchased the facility from the Walker brothers in 1890 and changed the name to the Moerlein-Gerst Brewing Co.

They hired J.C. Vaupel as manager, but Gerst moved to Nashville to brew the beer and oversee operations. Moerlein-Gerst specialized in the pilsner and lager styles of the owners' native region of Bavaria. Their initial brands were Old Jug Lager and Pilsener Export, products that would be flagships of the brewery for half a century. The company also bragged that it was the first brewery using stone bottles to package its beers, a claim that was only partially true since Moerlein's Cincinnati brewery was also shipping in stone crockware.

The sturdy stone bottles were manufactured in Glasgow, Scotland, and allowed for safer transportation of the beer. Previously, beer was shipped in kegs and then bottled closer to the ultimate consumer, but this development allowed breweries like Gerst to control their product throughout the logistics stream. The bottles were also suitable for bold imprinting and embossing, which served the dual purpose of advertising the brand and ensuring that

This postcard shows the massive scale of the William Gerst Brewing Company and advertises the brands produced there. *Courtesy of Scott Mertie.*

they would be returned to the proper brewery for reuse. These artistic packages are still much sought after by collectors.

Moerlein did not take an active role in managing his joint venture with Gerst and never moved from Cincinnati. So in March 1893, Gerst purchased Moerlein's share of the brewery and changed the name to the William Gerst Brewing Company. Gerst quickly added an Extra Pale Bohemian beer to the company's portfolio of products and aggressively began to market his company as "the largest and best equipped brewery in the South."

He saw the opportunity to educate new consumers who visited the state capital by exhibiting at the Tennessee State Fair, providing samples of his wares and even demonstrating his new bottling line at the German Village at the fairgrounds. His real chance to make a big splash came in 1897 when Tennessee celebrated one hundred years of statehood with the huge Centennial Exposition.

Held in what would become Centennial Park on the streetcar line that ran to the western edge of the city, the exposition grounds covered multiple acres. Many cities built their own exhibition halls, with Memphis acknowledging the Egyptian roots of the city's name with a huge pyramid and Nashville paying homage to its reputation as the "Athens of the South" by constructing a scale model of the Parthenon. This plaster monument was eventually replaced with a permanent version that still dominates Centennial Park today.

Other groups also built buildings and pavilions, and Gerst constructed a magnificent testament to his ambition. Gerst's pavilion featured a huge cask purported to hold 2,500 gallons of beer, a full demonstration bottling line and columns fashioned from hundreds of beer bottles. He also added a replica of an authentic *rathskeller*, a traditional German drinking hall that would be located in the basement of a civic building for the town council members to continue their discussions after adjournment over a stein of lager. Gerst's rathskeller was totally aboveground and served his Pilsener, Bohemian and an Extra Pale. There was also traditional German music to entertain the patrons.

Perhaps in part because of Gerst's glorious edifices—but most probably due to the quality of its beer—Gerst was awarded the gold medal at the Centennial Exposition, a fact that would be included in much of the brewery's advertising materials for decades. Like many successful breweries of the time (and since), Gerst believed strongly in the value of advertising. The company constantly produced tchotchkes like bottle openers, coasters, calendars and glasses emblazoned with the Gerst name to distribute to wholesale and retail customers across the South. The Gerst logo was a bold letter "G" wrapped around a dove to represent the pristine quality of their products. They also frequently made mention of the company's bottling line, a differentiating factor over competing distributors like Diehl and Lord, which were still being shipped in kegs for repackaging. Note that Diehl and Lord also built a grand pavilion at the Centennial Exposition but left without a gold medal.

The brewery is also known for its collectible advertising lithographs, colorful works of fine art that often featured paintings of beautiful women with no mention of beer at all, just the name of the brewery in script across the top of the piece. Eventually, Gerst would adopt the slogan "Brewed in Dixie" after the end of Prohibition to indicate its unique status as a large southern production brewery.

The production and reputation of Gerst continued to grow through the turn of the century, and William Gerst found himself prosperous enough to engage in a new hobby: horse racing. He built stables in South Nashville and began to raise thoroughbreds, several of which he raced in the prestigious Kentucky Derby in Louisville. In 1910, his horse Donau (named after the German name for the Danube River) won the Derby, becoming the only Tennessee-owned horse to win the Run for the Roses. A painting of the

The impressive Gerst Pavilion at the Centennial Exhibition was literally made from beer bottles and featured a 2,500-gallon cask of beer. *Courtesy of Scott Mertie, from the collection of Parthenon, Metro Parks.*

famous steed hung over William Gerst's desk at the brewery and is still on display at the Gerst Haus restaurant downtown.

The year 1910 was not a completely lucky one for Gerst—the man or the brewery—as Prohibition came to Tennessee ten years before the entire nation went dry. Just as the company was hitting its stride as a regional powerhouse, on July 1, 1910, the production of alcoholic beverages became illegal in the state of Tennessee.

Production at the facility frantically shifted to nonalcoholic beverages, placing the company at a decided disadvantage versus breweries in nearby "wet" states. The dove of the Gerst logo manifested itself as a brand in its line of Dove Pure Malt Beverages, which were touted as "the perfect drinks for home use," since the taverns and saloons had closed their doors with the advent of Prohibition. Gerst Select was a cereal beverage with malt, barley and hops that would now be considered a "near beer" with only .5 percent alcohol by volume.

Other nonalcoholic products released by Gerst during Prohibition included a Cola-Pepsin, named after an enzymatic additive that would later give its name to Pepsi Cola. Gerst also produced an Imperial Ginger Ale and other sodas. In an attempt to keep the production lines in use, Gerst began to bottle fruity Orange, Lime and Lemon Crushes, brands that are still popular in the South among soda lovers. Gerst also released a soda named Delaware Punch, a fruit soda named after Ohio's Delaware grape cultivar, not the Blue Hen State. Even after the repeal of national Prohibition in 1933, Gerst continued to distribute many of these nonalcoholic products.

Eventually, the grind of keeping the brewery running without being able to actually produce any beer drove William H. Gerst to retire back to Cincinnati in 1920. Fortunately, he had four sons who all worked with him in the operation and ran the business after his departure. The family patriarch passed away on March 10, 1933, and was buried in Spring Grove Cemetery, north of downtown Cincinnati. Regrettably, he did not live long enough to see his beloved brewery return to making beer after the official repeal of Prohibition just a month after his death.

As the first brewery in the state to officially register to reopen after the ratification of the Twenty-first Amendment, the Gerst sons hit the ground running and aggressively expanded Gerst's operations, adding a modern bottling line in 1934 that could process twenty six-packs per minute and reintroducing the famous recipe that had won the gold medal at the Centennial Exposition in 1897. They also raised the alcohol content of some of their brews as high as 6.25 percent in an attempt to attract pre-Prohibition drinkers back to the brand.

The brewery's fiftieth anniversary in 1940 was celebrated with extensive marketing efforts in newspapers all over the South thanking customers for their continued patronage. In addition to the "Brewed in Dixie" slogan, clever punny taglines began to appear in print ads. Gerst was promoted as "Always in Good Taste—Always Tastes Good" and as the "Thirst Choice for 50 Years," while drinkers were advised that "With Those Who Thirst, the Word is Gerst."

Production peaked at around 200,000 barrels per year, but large regional and national players were beginning to eat into Gerst's market share by the end of World War II. In recognition of the seemingly randomly selected fifty-seventh anniversary of the brewery in 1947, management decided to make another marketing push by renaming its signature pilsner beer as Gerst 57 Pilsner, having dropped the traditional first "e" in the German spelling of its flagship decades earlier. In another effort to recapture the sales that Pabst, Miller and Anheuser-Busch were siphoning away, Gerst released a new all-grain beer

Gerst 77 Extra Dry was one of the first canned products of the brewery available in distinctive "crowntainer" and "conetop" containers. *Courtesy of Scott Mertie.*

called King's Oasis, known as KO Ale for short. New doesn't always mean good, as the public greeted KO Ale with a resounding silence, and the brand quickly disappeared.

By 1950, the Gerst family could no longer afford to keep running the brewery and sold it to a group of local investors for the reported sum of $400,000. The new owners kept the name of the brewery and continued to manufacture some of the same brands as well as adding a new brew they called Gerst 77 Extra Dry beer. They also invested in Gerst's first canning line, offering 57 and 77 in "crowntainer" and "conetop" cans that could easily be mistaken for brake fluid vessels.

Gerst Brewery workers enjoy the last keg of beer produced in 1954. *Courtesy of Scott Mertie from the collection of the Nashville and Davidson County Archives.*

Sales still did not exceed expenses for the new operators of the Gerst Brewery, and in a last-ditch effort to boost the bottom line, it released two more new brands. Unlike the Old World lighter pilsners that earned the brewery its reputation over the years, Old Amber Premium Beer was a malty Oktoberfest-style brew that hit the market in 1952. The final product ever introduced by Gerst came out in 1953 with the release of Ten-E-Cee Hōm-Bru.

These new products didn't move the sales needle, and the owners of Gerst announced the brewery's imminent closing in 1954 with the final brewing occurring in February of that year. The brewery building remained vacant for several years until a Memphis company purchased it in 1957 to strip out the brewery equipment and sell much of it for scrap. The remainder of the building was used as a warehouse until the main brewhouse was demolished in 1963. The old three-story bottling building survived the wrecking ball and was used as a warehouse by an insulation company until it was destroyed by a fire in 1992 in a conflagration that could be seen as far away as Williamson County.

It's somehow appropriate that the final demise of the Gerst Brewery was visible for miles since, after sixty-four years of dominating the beer scene in Nashville, Gerst exerted an influence that was quite far-reaching. Part of the company and the family legacy would live on in the form of the Gerst Haus restaurant opened in 1955 by William H. Gerst's grandson, William J. Gerst. Although the restaurant has changed locations two times in the years since it first opened, it has always maintained a proximity to the courthouse, establishing itself as a popular meeting spot for attorneys, politicians and the journalists who cover them to share some afterhours conversation over German food and ice-cold beer served in huge fishbowl glasses.

In 1988, brothers Jim and Jerry Chandler purchased the Gerst Haus and contracted the Evansville Brewing Company in their hometown to produce a new version of Gerst Haus Premium Amber Beer, a nod to the original Gerst Old Amber. The beer became quite popular on draft, and in 1992, the brothers renamed it Gerst Amber and released it in bottles for the Tennessee and Indiana markets. Pittsburgh Brewing Company purchased Evansville Brewing in 1997 and shifted the product to its facility best known for brewing Iron City Beer. In 2011, local Nashville brewery Yazoo took over the production and marketing of Gerst Beer after many trial batches that convinced the Chandlers that the beloved Amber should return to its hometown.

CHAPTER 3

NASHVILLE'S BREWERY SCENE GOES DARK AND THE RISE OF THE "KILLER B'S"

"THE WAITING IS THE HARDEST PART"

After the William Gerst Brewing Company officially shut down production in 1954, the beer scene in Nashville became and remained rather desolate for more than thirty years. National players like Anheuser-Busch, Miller, Pabst and Schlitz took over the hearts and minds of Nashville drinkers, as well as the tap handles at local drinking establishments. During this period, Nashvillians became some of the highest per capita consumers of Budweiser products, a dubious distinction in the eyes of more refined beer fans and craft brewers to this day.

Perhaps the biggest beer news of this period was the expansion of Coors to Tennessee in the late '80s, making the bootlegging of the Banquet Beer that was glamorized in the iconic southern film *Smokey and the Bandit* unnecessary. The Boulder, Colorado–based brewery moved further to boost its exposure in Nashville by taking on the name sponsorship of the final Winston Cup race at the Nashville Fairgrounds Speedway, the Coors 420. Coors took advantage of its growing popularity in the Volunteer State by purchasing a former Stroh's brewing facility in Memphis in 1990. It ran the brewery where it produced Keystone Light and Zima until closing it in 2005.

So the door was wide open for any entrepreneurs who might want to brew a beer that demonstrated any level of complexity superior to the watery light lagers that had become the darlings of the uneducated palates of Nashvillians. Fortunately, a quartet of breweries stepped up between 1988 and 1997 to take advantage of the newly changed Tennessee laws

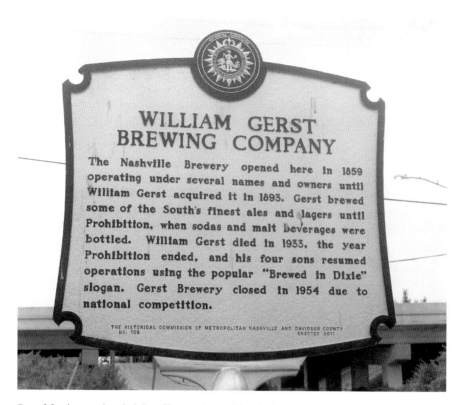

Scott Mertie spearheaded the effort to place a historical marker to mark the location of the former William Gerst Brewing Company at the corner of present-day Sixth Avenue South and Mulberry Street.

that allowed restaurants to brew beers on-premise. These four brewpubs could be called the "Killer B's." In chronological order, Bohannon Brewing Company, Blackstone Brewing Company, Boscos and Big River opened breweries that produced styles and quality of beers that were unfamiliar to most of a generation of Nashville residents.

Chapter 4

BOHANNON BREWING COMPANY/MARKET STREET PUB

"THE Y'ALL COME BACK SALOON"

Lindsay Bohannon was a Nashville businessman who was born in Bowling Green, Kentucky, and educated at Vanderbilt University. During a trip to Geissen, Germany, in the 1980s, Bohannon discovered a world of unfamiliar beers like hesse, dunkel and maibock. Upon returning home to the States, Bohannon decided to eschew the family tobacco business and start up his own brewery to introduce Nashville to new and interesting beers.

Brewpubs had not yet been legalized in the state, so brewing for distribution was Bohannon's only option. He exhibited an eye for history with his choice of a brewery site on Second Avenue North, the same address where two men named Crossman and Drucker had opened one of the city's first breweries in 1859. The actual building that housed Bohannon Brewing Company was constructed in 1888 as the warehouse for Tennessee's largest distillery of the day. Long before Mr. Jack Daniel dominated the spirits business in the state, another first-generation immigrant to Middle Tennessee named Charles Nelson shipped thousands of gallons of Nelson's Green Brier Tennessee Whiskey to markets ranging from Jacksonville, Florida, to San Francisco, California, to Paris, France, out of that warehouse via riverboats on the Cumberland River a block away.

The brewery that Bohannon constructed in 1988 had a capacity of 2,500 barrels per year, fairly large for a microbrewery but dwarfed by the huge commercial breweries that still dominated the industry. Recognizing that local beer drinkers needed to be spoon-fed with the idea of craft beers,

Bohannon produced a broad spectrum of easy-drinking brews, plus some flavored specialty styles to appeal to a wider range of tastes. Bohannon's novel method of cold filtration instead of pasteurization was also a selling point for the beers.

Particularly popular was his Nut Brown Ale, a mahogany-colored English-style ale that was brewed with roasted barley, Perle and Cascade hops and five different types of malts: two-row pale, victory, carapils, caramel and chocolate. The resulting nutty brown ale fairly flew out the door after Bohannon started bottling and established the company's reputation as a serious brewer. This reputation was reaffirmed in 1989 when its Market Street Oktoberfest won a gold medal in the Vienna/Märzen/Oktoberfest category of the Great American Beer Festival. Named after the original designation of Second Avenue where the brewery was located, the Market Street moniker became the brand that Bohannon released future products under and the name of the brewpub that would eventually be constructed at the brewery site.

Other styles of beer that Bohannon released included traditional draft and light pilsners, golden ales, winter lagers, porters, hefeweizens, Bavarian wheats and a bock beer. Bohannon wasn't afraid of a good (or bad) pun and gave a nod to the Music City heritage of his brewery with releases called Jailhouse Bock and Cole Porter Stout. Also well received were a Blackberry Wheat and a Vanilla Cream Ale that many beer fans in Nashville still remember fondly as their gateway into craft beers. Over the years, Bohannon Brewing Company garnered more than forty medals at various national beer competitions.

Within the first year of opening the brewery, Bohannon saw that his sales were already above his initial projections and expanded distribution to include markets outside of Nashville, including his hometown of Bowling Green. At its peak, the brewery's products were available in bottles in eleven states.

When the Tennessee legislature legalized brewpubs in 1993, Lindsay Bohannon saw the opportunity to expand his customer base and take advantage of his location in Nashville's tourist district. He opened Market Street Brewery and Public House in 1994, serving nine of his beers on tap to crowds of thirsty patrons while filling them up with a menu of upscale pub grub and southern specialty foods.

Not only did this demonstrate bravery to open a restaurant on top of the already new and unproven concept of a microbrewery, but the building that housed Market Street was also rumored to be haunted. Chairs were purported to move across the floors with no human assistance, light switches flipped on or off by themselves and chandeliers swung back and forth without the presence of any wind. The building is still a popular stop on historical ghost tours of Nashville.

After a good run through the turn of the twentieth century, Bohannon found the dynamics of the brewing industry were putting too much pressure on his enterprise and made the difficult decision to cease operations at the brewery in January 2004. The restaurant side of Market Street stayed open for another two years until Bohannon sold the building to a Savannah, Georgia–based development firm for $3.2 million. The developers, in turn, flipped the building to New York–based East Coast Saloons. Among the restaurant concepts developed by East Coast Saloons was McFadden's Restaurant and Pub, which they chose to open in the former Bohannon location in 2007.

Although his career as a brewer and restaurateur was relatively short, Lindsay Bohannon is remembered as a key player in the development of Nashville's craft brewing industry and an early activist in the business development of the city's bourgeoning Lower Broad commercial district.

CHAPTER 5

BLACKSTONE BREWING COMPANY

"BLACK WATER"

Nashville's first brewpub was a game changer, and it was founded by two passionate people whose complementary talents combined for success in the face of great obstacles. Confronted by a Nashville market that was in the middle of a restaurant boom and a predilection for, ahem, less full-flavored beers, Blackstone Restaurant & Brewery had a rocky path to navigate, but Kent Taylor and Stephanie Weins possessed the skills and dedication to make it work.

Taylor, an accountant by trade, didn't even like craft beer when the concept of opening a brewpub was first presented to him. During the late 1980s, a friend and client named Hank Williams (not the country musician but still an important figure in Music City, nonetheless) was discussing potential retirement plans with Taylor and invited him to be involved in the project: "In twenty years, we will sell our businesses, move to Seattle and open a brewpub." Taylor didn't even know what a brewpub was, but the idea sounded appealing.

Another friend, James Callahan, worked for Cumberland Beverage, the distributor that initially brought Coors to Nashville. Having attended a private Church of Christ school for college, Taylor wasn't really much of a beer drinker, but Callahan wanted to introduce his friend to the wonderful world of craft beer. Callahan was instrumental in convincing Cumberland to represent some of the first microbrews in town and was excited to offer Kent his first Anchor Steam beer.

"I couldn't even finish it," Taylor recalls. "It was too bitter for me, but it did pique my interest." One of the only other craft beers that was available in Nashville was the Guinness served in huge cans at his local Irish pub. He said, "All I could get was Triple Stout, so I definitely cut my teeth on full-flavored beers." Taylor was hooked and began to read every book he could get his hands on to learn more about beer. Williams encouraged Kent to start homebrewing, and the bookish Taylor dove into the hobby with more research and practice batches.

Around this same time in 1991, Taylor met a woman who would change the direction of his life. Stephanie Weins was working as the manager of a restaurant client of Taylor's firm. When the owner of the downtown eatery decided to sell the business, Kent suggested that he and Stephanie should raise the money to buy it or open their own place. A food service veteran, Weins told Kent that she didn't want to be married to the restaurant business since it promised a life of knocking your head against the wall trying to accomplish the same thing that every other restaurateur was attempting. Still, the seed had been planted.

In 1992, Callahan decided to open up his own beer distributorship to concentrate on craft products for the Nashville market. He needed a business address for his license, so Taylor offered up his conference room as the official locale of Community Beverage Company. While he managed his own accounting firm, Taylor saw the ins and outs of the beer biz as Callahan worked under the same roof.

In 1993, Callahan walked into the office with a copy of the new legislation legalizing brewpubs in Tennessee. Suddenly, the prospect of opening a restaurant got a lot more interesting to Taylor and Weins. Taylor says, "She saw the opportunity to differentiate our place from everybody else. The idea of offering a unique product could make all the effort worthwhile." Nashville was an underserved restaurant market in the early '90s, but competition was booming with more than two hundred other dining spots opening within two years of Taylor and Weins swinging open the doors of their brewpub.

The couple undertook a crash course in the business of brewing, with Taylor ramping up his homebrewing to experiment with new recipes and styles of beer, immersing himself in every book and magazine he could get his hands on and both of them visiting all the brewpubs within driving distance and several others that required air travel.

Taylor and Weins had more work to do than just drinking great beer across the country, though. There was the small matter of acquiring the financing to buy the brewing equipment and build a restaurant. Thanks to his experience working with business accounting, Taylor knew that "at that time, it wasn't a bankable business. We needed investor financing." Calls

Blackstone Restaurant & Brewery enjoys a prime location in the West End in the heart of Nashville's Midtown.

to just about everyone they knew led to no nibbles. They needed an actual building site to make it real to potential partners.

Taylor knew about a location in the heavily traveled Midtown section of West End Avenue and found a partner who was willing to buy the property, invest in improvements and lease it back to them as restaurant tenants. At that point, the clock was ticking to raise the rest of the money to open up their dream business.

Taylor convinced Weins to make the jump. He says, "We had ninety days to raise $1 million. We scraped together everything we had and maxed out our credit cards to get the $20,000 in earnest money. If we couldn't put together the rest of the financing within three months, we would have lost it all. Everybody said we were crazy and would be closed within six months."

Two months of scrambling resulted in no investors, but finally a local venture capitalist expressed interest and suggested another potential partner in Kansas City. After a presentation of their business plan to the out-of-state investor led to an agreement, the venture went from 0 to 80 percent funded in a week. Kent's brother Todd came in for the balance of the loan, and the brewpub was many steps closer to becoming a reality.

Taylor had won medals for his homebrewing prowess, but he recognized that they would need a professional brewmaster. Dave Miller literally wrote the book on homebrewing with his manual *The Complete Handbook of Home Brewing* and through his regular troubleshooting column in *Brewing Techniques* magazine. On a research visit to the St. Louis Brewery and Taproom, Taylor saw a copy of Miller's book on sale and suddenly realized that "Dr. Dave" actually worked there. Despite the fact that he already owned a dog-eared copy of the book, Taylor immediately bought another one and asked Miller to autograph it for him. The two brewers spent more than an hour discussing the brewpub business, touring the brewery and talking about their philosophies of beer making. Taylor returned to Nashville invigorated and inspired by the man he considered his "brew god."

So when Taylor and Weins closed on their real estate deal in February 1994, Kent's first move was to write a letter to Miller to inquire if he knew where they might find a brewer for their new business. To Taylor's surprise, Miller called him back the evening that he received the letter to express his own interest in the position. Miller had retired after fifteen years as a brewer at the brewpub in St. Louis and after winning numerous national awards for his beers, but he was convinced to come out of retirement and move his wife and five children to Nashville to throw their lot in with Taylor and Weins. It didn't hurt that Miller's wife's sister lived in Nashville.

The brewing equipment had already been ordered from Century Brewing Systems of Ohio by the summer of '94, thanks to more of Taylor's obsessively fastidious research, but there was still time for Miller to tweak the specs a bit. Although Century has since gone out of business, its equipment is still coveted for its reliability and quality construction. The original system was a fifteen-barrel brewhouse with a two-vessel system featuring a combination mash/lauter tun and a kettle/whirlpool, plus a separate hot liquor tank. The brewing area was designed to compactly fit four fifteen-barrel fermentation tanks, five fifteen-barrel bright tanks and a thirty-barrel bright tank that would allow the pub side of the brewpub to serve its beer directly from those tanks.

The one thing the brewpub did not have at this point was a name. With concrete and steel already in the ground on West End Avenue, Taylor and Weins knew they had to come up with something to put up on a sign in front. They put out the word to their friends that they would offer free beer for a year to whoever came up with a winning name for the brewpub. The nine-year-old nephew of one of Kent's clients offered up the name Blackstone. Taylor wanted a British-sounding name to describe the pubby environment

The small brewhouse at Blackstone produces beer for use in the brewpub.

that he had imagined, and Blackstone fit the bill quite nicely since William Blackstone was the eighteenth-century British jurist who codified the system of common law that is the basis of many countries' judicial systems. Weins eventually acquired the honorary quasi-British title of "Lady Blackstone."

Although the nine-year-old didn't get the beer, his mother took advantage of the offer to throw a party at the new pub to burn through the whole year's worth for her and her friends in one evening. Taylor actually ran into the young man years later while on vacation in Panama City Beach. When he complimented the apparent stranger on his snappy Blackstone T-shirt, the boy replied, "I named that place."

Miller brewed several test batches to calibrate the equipment and zero in on the recipes that he and Taylor had chosen to feature, and Blackstone Restaurant & Brewery was ready to open on New Year's Eve 1994. Nashville was still a market that was relatively unfamiliar with craft beers since even Bohannon's distribution of bottled products was primarily outside the city. Taylor remembers, "At first, the public questioned why we didn't have their favorite domestic beers on tap, but we remained committed to only serving our own beers. In the face of all the other restaurant competition, we couldn't have survived without the beer."

Blackstone's initial offering was planned to be three core recipes and three rotating "brewmaster's specials" from the notebooks of Miller. The brews that were always on tap were Chaser Pale, a German-style ale called a kölsch that Taylor brewed with and named after Weins's son Chase; Red Springs Ale, an American amber; and St. Charles Porter, a British brown porter named after Taylor's son. Of the initial rotating seasonals and specials like oatmeal stout and an Oktoberfest märzen, the one that really took off was an English brown called Blackstone Nut Brown Ale. It was quickly added to the list of core beers, and the number of brewmaster's specials was reduced to two.

The core list of beers stayed the same for more than four years when Blackstone American Pale Ale supplanted Red Springs on the brewpub's tap handles. Miller is a big fan of lagers, but Taylor loves ales. Determined to stay true to his preferences and to educate Nashville's drinking community, Taylor kept the focus of the brewery on his beloved ales. But the team did work collaboratively to develop new recipes, including the occasional pilsner or lager for the brewpub. Miller had no desire to experiment with Belgian beers, but Weins challenged him to try it. So Miller went all the way with it to brew a popular malty dubbel ale that he named Stephanie's Dubbel in her honor.

Taylor didn't feel like their beer was ready for brewing competitions yet, so they waited until 1996 to enter their first brews in the World Beer Cup and the Great American Beer Festival (GABF). Blackstone earned medals in both competitions and has enjoyed success in contests ever since. In fact, St. Charles Porter ranks fourth on the list of the most-medaled beers in the history of the GABF with eight awards over the years. Still actively involved in his own accounting business, eventually Taylor had to stop attending the October awards ceremony in Denver to pick up Blackstone's awards since October 15 is the final deadline for his many clients who procrastinate until the late filing date.

Business at the brewery continued to grow as the locals began to discover the joys of locally made craft beers. In 1997, Blackstone hired Travis Hixon as an additional brewer. Taylor had always had an eye on distributing Blackstone's beers outside of the brewery to be able to share his products with more people, and the brewery began to keg a few beers to dip its toes in the self-distribution biz. He even made a run at a potential production brewery location on Clifton Avenue in West Nashville in 2003, but it would be most of a decade before that vision became a reality.

When Bohannon and Market Street shut down, there was a real opportunity to get into the packaging business, but Blackstone didn't have the room or the compunction to add a bottling line to the brewpub. In 2005, Taylor contracted with Frederick Brewing Co. in Maryland to use some of its excess capacity to brew and bottle Chaser Pale and Nut Brown Ale. Frederick was chosen because it was willing to allow Blackstone's brewers to be on site to oversee the brewing process and quality control. Every month, one member of the staff would fly to the East Coast for brew day, and the resulting products became very popular in Nashville, ranking number two to Sierra Nevada in craft brew sales.

Unfortunately, Frederick Brewing Co. sold out to Flying Dog in 2006, and the new owners cancelled all their brewing contracts. Having had a taste of the possibilities of the distribution business, Taylor and Weins decided to bring the operation in house and get serious about a new production facility. They formulated a new business plan and went in search of more financing, this time in the form of a Small Business Administration 504 loan.

Financing was arranged, and they were due to close on September 15, 2008. This turned out to be an inopportune date as it was the day that Lehman Brothers declared bankruptcy and the Dow Jones lost almost five hundred points. Needless to say, their financiers got cold feet, and the deal was scuttled. Blackstone's owners contacted every bank they could think of over most of the next year for support on the 504 loan until they eventually attracted the interest of a small financial institution in Clarksville named First Advantage Bank that would eventually become Avenue Bank based out of Nashville. Taylor, Weins and Miller wooed the bank's decision makers at the brewpub, and the bank finally came on board with the project.

With financing in place, Taylor started to source the equipment for Blackstone's new facility, even without a building location yet chosen. The day that their deal with the bank was approved in July 2009, Taylor made an offer on a retired bottling line that Magic Hat Brewery in Burlington, Vermont, had been trying to sell for almost a year. He offered half of the asking price, and the brewery took it, causing Taylor to curse himself for leaving money on the table. While it was still expensive to rehab and move the bottling line, it was a solid piece of equipment with a capacity of one hundred bottles per minute from sixteen filling heads.

Even more valuable was the week that Taylor spent in Burlington disassembling and packing up the line. Although he wouldn't have anywhere to reassemble the machine for more than a year, Taylor was worried about leaving his new acquisition on the floor of another brewery. When he arrived at Magic Hat, he was daunted at the prospect of taking apart the complex mechanism and called Weins in distress. She told him to

Blackstone's large production brewery facility opened at 2312 Clifton Avenue in 2011.

The large, modern brewhouse at Blackstone brews beer for distribution in bottles as well as contract brewing for Schlafly and Falls City.

just do it one piece at a time, and Taylor and a companion spent six days from 9:00 a.m. until 1:00 a.m. breaking down and crating up the line. Ever the meticulous researcher, he seized the opportunity to learn about every little piece of the bottling line and collect and read every manual that could teach him about its operation.

After returning to Nashville, it was time to set about finding a place to actually build a production brewery. Taylor inquired about a large tract of land, again on Clifton Avenue, but soon decided that it would have to be subdivided to make it economically feasible. He next called about that original piece of property next door that he had first looked at in 2003. The motivated seller took his first offer for the property, again leaving Taylor grumbling about his negotiating skills.

Without extra funding to hire a building designer, Taylor taught himself computer-aided design (CAD) software and drew up his own plans for the facility to be approved and redrafted by licensed engineers. For the dream brewhouse in his new facility, Taylor spent six days in California observing the German-made Rolak system at Lagunitas Brewing Company in Petaluma. He decided on a 30-barrel, four-vessel system from Rolak paired with five 30-barrel fermenters, five 60-barrel fermenters, one 60-barrel bright tank and one 120-barrel bright tank, all from JWNW of Oregon.

He began to price out the construction of the building, and all of the bids came in too high for his liking. A quote of $175,000 for an air-conditioned office and tasting room caused Taylor to ask himself, "Will this make the beer any better?" His answer was no, and those amenities were axed from the plans. He did install the first actual laboratory in a brewery in the state to ensure quality control for his products.

Construction was completed in the spring of 2011, and in May, the first kegs of Blackstone beer rolled out of the production facility. July of that year was to be a bittersweet month for the partners of Blackstone. On July 25, the first bottles from their packaging line shipped to Nashville stores to the elation of Taylor and Weins. Tragically, the very next day, Weins was diagnosed with stage-four lung cancer. While still reeling with this bleak outlook for the future, Taylor and Weins visited their local pharmacy to pick up her first course of prescriptions to fight the disease. While walking in the grocery aisle holding a bag full of medications, the couple turned the corner to see a stack of six-packs of their products featured prominently in the store's beer section and Scott Turner of their distribution partner Ajax Turner happily introducing customers to the new opportunity to enjoy a locally brewed craft beer at home.

Despite the pessimistic diagnosis of her original oncologist, Weins outlived her expected lifespan by years, finally passing away on Valentine's Day 2014. The local craft beer community was rocked by the loss, and Taylor set up a charitable opportunity called Stephanie's Fight to raise money to fund nonprofit lung cancer research programs. A special brew of a high-gravity American Double/Imperial Stout called Black Belle Imperial Stout was brewed in March 2014 in Stephanie's honor with proceeds contributed to the charity's efforts.

Life goes on without Weins at both the brewpub and production brewery, but her presence is still in the hearts of many people who drink or work there. The brewery on Clifton continues to expand, adding tanks to increase potential annual production capacity to almost fifteen thousand barrels. Blackstone has taken on a few contract brewing projects to fill up its tanks while still allowing flexibility for its own production growth. On Fridays, Blackstone produces the wash, or fermented grain product prior to distillation, that Nashville distillery Popcorn Sutton uses to make its Tennessee White Whiskey. Blackstone also brews products for Falls City, a popular Louisville-based brewery that has reintroduced its brands after closing down the original brewery in 1978.

To accommodate the added production needs of Falls City, Blackstone convinced the company to purchase three new tanks that increased the facility's fermenting capacity by 60 percent. In turn, Blackstone leases the tanks back from Falls City and will own them outright at the completion of the term of their contract together.

The contract brewing partnership that has earned the greatest acclaim for Blackstone is its agreement to brew kegged British-style pale ale for Schlafly, another respected craft brewer out of St. Louis that also just happens to be a former employer of brewmaster Dave Miller. Taylor is proud of the association. He says, "It's a balancing act between their beer and ours. We don't treat Schlafly's products any different from our own, and we contribute the same passion to the brewing. That's why they like us."

Since Schlafly brews and produces its own version of Schlafly's Pale Ale, it was critical to be able to match the flavor profiles between the two breweries. That's where that laboratory comes in handy. Taylor says, "We've got a great relationship with Schlafly, and we both hold each other to extremely high standards, even when they are not physically here during brewing."

Blackstone was also the first brewery in the state to receive a distillery license to brew high-gravity beers like its popular Adam Bomb IPA. Future planned offerings include a chocolate milk stout and continued expansion of

Kent Taylor has a large garden behind the brewing facility in addition to an expansive complex for growing different varieties of hops.

its seasonal specials, like its fall Pumpkin Ale and summer Picnic, a lighter version of a classic English pale ale.

Distribution could expand further within the current footprint where Blackstone is sold in every major market of Tennessee with the exception of Jackson. Taylor is cautious, though, saying, "We love the Chattanooga and Knoxville markets and would like to sell even more there. But we're scared to talk to them in case they start to order more!" More tanks are on order, but the next expansion will have to involve blowing out the back wall of the production facility, an eventuality that Taylor built into his original plans. With available property behind the brewery ready to be built on, Blackstone's future as a dominant Tennessee brewer is assured. Having already shipped the millionth bottle out of the facility in 2012, the market's thirst for its products still seems unquenchable.

CHAPTER 6

BOSCOS PIZZA KITCHEN AND BREWERY

"MEMPHIS IN THE MEANTIME"

Tennessee's first brewpub actually opened in Memphis in 1992. The state legislature, led by Memphis senator Steve Cohen, repealed a policy dating back to Prohibition requiring that the distribution chain for alcoholic products maintain a separation between manufacturers, distributors and retail sales outlets. In a brewpub environment, all three roles are played by a single entity, and taxes must be paid at each level.

Two Memphis businessmen, Jerry Steinhouse and Chuck Skypeck, took immediate advantage of the law change and opened up Boscos Pizza Kitchen and Brewery in December 1992, just six months after their proposed venture became legal. Neither man had any experience in the restaurant or commercial brewing industry, with Steinhouse spending his professional career in finance as a stockbroker and Skypeck making his living as a drugstore manager.

But they both had dreams of moving into new professions and came together to combine Steinhouse's desire to open a pizza café and Skypeck's concept of expanding his homebrewing experience into a full-scale brewery. Skypeck started homebrewing in 1984 and had visited more than two hundred breweries and brewpubs during the decade before Boscos opened in the name of "research." The two founders agreed that their venture must have a dual focus on both quality food and well-crafted beer, shortcomings that Skypeck had encountered in many of the visits that he had made on his grand tour of American brewpubs.

Boscos opened in the tony Germantown neighborhood east of downtown Memphis with a small seven-barrel brewhouse and a book of Skypeck's

The cramped brewroom at Boscos is located on the second floor of the restaurant, in view of dining and drinking patrons.

homebrew recipes that he had developed over the years. In addition to wood-fired pizzas and upscale pub fare, the plan was for Boscos to feature four core beers and at least four other seasonals and special recipes on tap.

Memphis took quickly to the new concept, and after four years of steady growth, Skypeck and Steinhouse looked east to expand to Nashville. They ordered an almost identical brewing system to install in a Hillsboro Village building that had formerly housed two quirky restaurants named the Flying Fish and Multi Bob and in the distant past was the location of the neighborhood Woolworth's.

With soaring ceilings and a popular bar inside the front door, it's easy to be distracted and not even notice the brewhouse tucked in the back of the dining room behind a window on the second floor. Compact and specifically designed for restaurant use, the totally manual seven-barrel brewing system feeds into six fermentation tanks sized to fit the brew kettle. Beer is then pumped upstairs to nine serving tanks that feed by gravity to the taps at the bar.

Since the Nashville Boscos only brews for internal use at the restaurant, this small efficient system works well for the company and allows for lots of flexibility and experimentation when it comes to new recipes. Despite running through as many as fifty different types of beer in a year, current head brewer Karen Lassiter is proud that she's never had an empty tank. "We've been here so long," she relates. "Patterns have been established, so you just have to get into a groove." Boscos usually brews twice a week, spending the other days cleaning the system and transferring beer between tanks.

Skypeck moved to Nashville as the original brewer at the Hillsboro Village location, transferring the Memphis brewing duties to Jimmy Randall, who is still with the company as the head brewer of its production brewery that goes by the name of Ghost River Brewing Company. He brought his recipes with him from the Bluff City and began to introduce Nashvillians to Boscos' core products. His first brew was a light-bodied Tennessee Cream Ale, an easy drinking beer with hints of malt and cream.

The four core beers featured at Boscos are not necessarily the same at each of its locations in Memphis, Nashville and Little Rock. All of the brewpubs feature Boscos' signature beer, Famous Flaming Stone Beer. Brewed using an ancient German method that includes superheating a large piece of pink granite in the restaurant's wood ovens and lowering it into the vessel during the brewing process, Flaming Stone benefits from the caramelizing that takes place during the contact of the beer and the hot stone. At the Nashville location, brewers don't completely wash the granite between brews, which allows for even more smoky caramelized character to be imparted to the beer.

In the old days, British brewers used to add extra hops as a preservative to the beers that they shipped to their colonies in the Far East. Not only did this prevent spoilage in the extreme temperatures of India, but it also created an intensely hoppy beer to the delight of colonial drinkers. Boscos Bombay IPA is an homage to this style, and the amber beer is a favorite of local "hopheads."

Isle of Sky Scottish Ale is the third core beer at Boscos Nashville. Made with seven different types of malt and three varieties of hops, this dark copper-colored ale is a rich full-bodied brew with great complexity and a hint of vanilla on the finish.

The final core product is Hillsboro Brown, a traditional English-style nut ale made with chocolate malt to contribute the nuttiness that makes it an extremely food-friendly beer. As the local name indicates, Hillsboro Brown is a Nashville brand, though a very similar brew is available under different names at other locations. When British beer expert Michael Jackson visited Boscos in 1999, he commented that Nashville's version of the IPA did not taste the same as the IPA he had sampled in Memphis. Fred Scheer, the brewer at the time, asked, "Why should it?" Jackson approved of the answer, and Boscos is proud of the fact that the local water, brewing environment and individual styles and talents of its brewers are allowed to shine through at each location.

All four of Boscos' core beers have medaled at either the Great American Beer Festival or the Real Ale Festival, and the talented brewers who have rotated through the brewhouse at the Nashville location are constantly coming up with new and interesting recipes. After four years starting up the Hillsboro Village Boscos, Skypeck handed off the reins to Fred Scheer in April 2000. Scheer was a veteran brewer from Germany with decades of experience, including an education at the DOEMENS Academy of Brewing and Malting in Munich. Scheer brought an important outsider's perspective to Boscos and encouraged even more experimentation in its roster of non-core beers.

Some of the notable specials and seasonals that make their way through the rotation include Olde Fool, an English strong ale with intense hops and malt flavors plus a hint of fruitiness; Westbound and Brown, a nutty brown ale made with three hop varieties; and HopGod Ale, an intensely hoppy American IPA with strong citrus notes. Local homebrewer Thomas Vista, who goes by the same nickname as the beer, developed the recipe for HopGod, and author Randy Mosher featured the recipe in his book *Extreme Brewing*.

Scheer always encouraged homebrewers to use Boscos as a home base for club meetings and was happy to interact with them and play with their recipes. Boscos still sponsors a yearly Pro/Am brewing competition as part of National Homebrew Day, an official American Homebrewers Association event. The Big Brew takes place the first Saturday of May in Boscos' parking lot. The brewery provides a common wort for all the amateur brewers who assemble their equipment in the back lot and brew up their own individual batches. The head brewer of Boscos joins with a lucky selected customer to choose his or her favorite recipe from the contestants. The brewpub then produces a full brew of the winning recipe to serve on tap in the bar and to enter into the national AHA competition.

One of the members of the homebrew club who used to hang around the bar at Boscos to enjoy its beers and learn from Scheer was Karen Lassiter. After leaving her longtime position in the printing industry in 2007, Lassiter found it difficult to find another job in her trade. She took that as a sign that perhaps she could consider a career change. Thanks to recognition at various competitions, her three years of hobby brewing seemed like a good background to launch a new vocation. She decided to further her education in the industry by taking a correspondence course from the Siebel Institute of Technology in Chicago.

Realizing that she needed more hands-on experience in a production brewery, Lassiter apprenticed for a few months under Travis Hixon at Blackstone. When that term was over, she approached Scheer to continue her education. She says, "Fred's an old-school German, and he said no to the apprenticeship. So I went over his head and e-mailed Chuck for a job."

Skypeck surprised Lassiter by also denying the apprenticeship but instead offering her a full-time job as assistant brewer under Scheer. She learned from her mentor for a year until Scheer left Boscos to help out with a start-up brewery venture in Franklin. Lassiter likes to brew more traditional English and European styles at Boscos, but personally she's a fan of new American-style ales with intense, high-acid hops. Her KPA (Karen's Pale Ale) is one of her favorite special beers and a popular expression of her taste for Citra hops.

Each location of Boscos sources its own supplies of hops and malt, so availability can sometimes be problematic, like during the Great Hops Shortage of 2009. More popular and exotic hops like Amarillo, Citra and some of the products from Australia and New Zealand are not always available consistently, but Lassiter does like to play with them when she has access. She says, "I understand the need to bring in new customers and appeal to less adventurous drinkers, but my husband and I are real hopheads!" Together with new assistant brewer Jim Craig, Lassiter hopes to incorporate even more of her homebrewing recipes into the brewery's rotating roster.

Since Boscos already has a liquor license for the bar, it hopes to be able to experiment with high-gravity beers in the future, but Lassiter does have concerns that their small mash tun capacity might be problematic, since high gravs require more malt and grains to feed the extra fermentation.

Another specialty at Boscos is its line of cask-conditioned beers, made using traditional British methods. After primary fermentation, the beer is moved to kegs for secondary fermenting and conditioning in the vessel that allows for natural carbonation. The beer is served unfiltered with live yeast still contained in the glass and is referred to as "real ale" for this reason. It is also dispensed through what Boscos calls its "beer engine," a device that pumps the beer from the keg to the glass without the use of extra gas pressure.

The cask-conditioned beers are special editions of the regular recipes from the brewery and change at least weekly. Every weekday evening at five-thirty, a lucky bar patron is selected as the "daily cellarman." The

Boscos' head brewer, Karen Lassiter, supervises the pouring of the day's cask-conditioned beer employing the brewery's English-style beer machine.

A lucky bar patron is named as the "daily cellarman" and gets to tap the day's selection of cask-conditioned ales.

customer has the privilege of tapping that day's special brew, enjoying the first pint and the chance to win a trip to represent the brewpub at the Great American Beer festival.

For a low-volume brewery, Boscos produces a dizzying array of interesting brews, necessitating frequent visits to ensure that beer enthusiasts don't miss out on something new before it passes out of the tanks and off the taps. Make sure to get there around 5:00 p.m. if you want a chance to knock the bung out of the firkin and get the first crack at that day's special.

Chapter 7

BIG RIVER GRILLE AND BREWING WORKS/ROCK BOTTOM RESTAURANT AND BREWERY

"ROLLIN' ON THE RIVER"

Like Boscos, the fourth "Killer B" of Nashville brewpubs also originated somewhere else in the state besides Music City. The original Big River Grille opened at 222 Broad Street in Chattanooga in 1996. The company was started by restaurateur Tim Hennen along with a group of investors, including Allen Corey, Jon Kinsey and Rob Gentry. Even with the 1992 law change to allow brewpubs in Tennessee, legal codes still required that a brewpub operate in a city with at least one million residents in the Metropolitan Statistical Area, so Chattanooga didn't qualify. Hennen and Gentry spent months lobbying the legislature to modify that codicil before they could officially begin brewing in their facility.

The brewpub opened with four beers on tap: a wheat, an amber, a pale ale and a stout. Since it had been decades since most Chattanoogans had tried anything other than a light lager, the staff at Big River offered free samplers of all four varieties in an effort to educate the palates of their patrons. The investment in free beer paid off with rapid growth, and soon the investors began to eye Nashville for possible expansion.

Gentry and his brother Clay opened the second outpost of Big River Grille and Brewing works in 1997 at the foot of Lower Broad within a block of where the, well, big river Nashvillians call the Cumberland flows through downtown. In the 1990s, the first five or six blocks of Broadway was still a rather seedy area with adult bookstores and theaters interspersed

Rock Bottom Restaurant and Brewery is located at the foot of Broadway, right in the middle of Nashville's popular tourist district.

with feed stores and warehouses. One of those old warehouses became home to Big River. Current manager John Burgess recalls, "Things were really different back then. The Hard Rock Café was still a Porter Paints store, and we used to buy rolled oats for some of our brews at Acme Feed Supply next door."

The Gentrys brought their original recipes with them up Interstate 24 along with Lance Roy, the original brewer who would man the tanks at the Nashville Big River for twelve years. The facility installed a brewery system fabricated by Specific Mechanical Systems out of Vancouver. A two-vessel, ten-barrel brewhouse fed into four ten-barrel fermenters in the cramped brewing room visible behind glass in the middle of the restaurant area behind the long L-shaped bar. In May 2013, the open fermenters were swapped for five twenty-barrel unitanks that allow for fermentation and aging in the same tank. The finished beer flows by gravity into the basement of the building into twelve ten-barrel dish-bottom serving and lagering tanks for storage. Carbon dioxide–driven peristaltic pumps drive the beer back upstairs at fifty-five psi into the taps at the bar, including all the way to the new rooftop bar area that was added in April 2013.

The crowded brewhouse at Rock Bottom is situated in the middle of the restaurant and is visible through large windows.

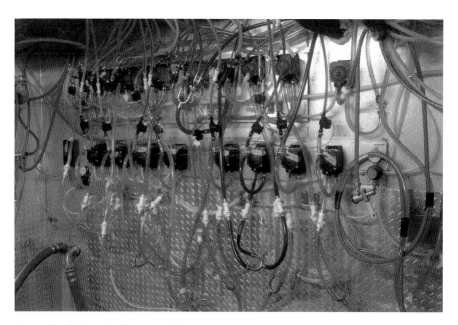

A complicated tangle of tanks and lines distributes Rock Bottom's beers to the bar and the rooftop deck.

Soon the brewery added new varieties of beers, including some lighter, more familiar styles to appeal to Bud/Miller/Coors drinkers. By far, the most popular beer among the novice drinkers was Southern Flyer Light Lager, a low-alcohol (2.7 percent ABV) golden American lager made with Liberty hops. Other Nashville brands of the early years of Big River included Metro Nut Brown Ale, a light-bodied ale made with chocolate malts, and the more aggressive Iron Horse Stout, with a thick, creamy head and roasted malt flavors and Fuggle hops. Big River's red ale went by the name of Thick Brick Ale and appealed more to the beer connoisseur than the casual drinker.

Patrons also enjoyed a cask-conditioned Blue Star made with floral Mount Hood hops. The brewery's Sixteenth Avenue Pilsner was a lager that gave a nod to Nashville's songwriting community with its geographic shout out of a name to the address of many publishing companies on Music Row. Nashville Steamer was a golden ale made from honey malt and a large dose of Cascade hops for an aggressive attack on the palate.

Big River opened two more locations in Greenville, South Carolina, and at the Boardwalk Resort at Walt Disney World before a big change came that would mean the end of expansion under the brewpub's original name. In 1999, Big River's parent company acquired the much-larger Gordon Biersch chain of brewpubs based out of Palo Alto, California. The combined company took on the name of the new acquisition but continued to run out of Chattanooga. Future openings of new brewpubs took on the Gordon Biersch brand name. The company also formed a joint venture with another national brewpub operator, Rock Bottom Brewery, to open and operate new locations around the Southeast.

Business continued to grow as Lower Broad cleaned up its act and became more of a tourist destination throughout the first decade of the twenty-first century. Hans Johnson replaced Roy as head brewer after twelve years and served in that capacity until 2008. Johnson was previously the opening brewmaster for Babe's Bar-B-Que & Brewhouse in Rancho Mirage, California, in 2002 and won many awards during his tenure there, including GABF, Australian International, California State Fair and World Beer Cup medals. After leaving Big River, Johnson moved on to Blackstone for a period and then into private consulting, where he now helps to start up new breweries and troubleshoot existing operations.

Brad Mortensen took over the brew kettle after Johnson's departure and still serves in that capacity. Mortensen was a homebrewer until taking on the brewing job at Potomac River Brewing for two and a half years starting in 1996. After that brewery was sold, Mortensen moved to Legend Brewery in

These lagering tanks in the basement of Rock Bottom were completely flooded and left floating during the Great Flood of 2010.

Richmond, Virginia, to take the job as assistant brewer in 1998. After just six months, the head brewer quit, and Mortensen ascended to the top job at the longtime Virginia favorite.

Eight years later, Mortensen jumped at the opportunity to start up a new brewery named Old Harbor in San Juan, Puerto Rico. When his two-year contract was up, Mortensen left the island behind and came to Nashville to lead the brewing efforts at Big River during a very important transitional time.

He was also at the helm when the big flood of May 2010 hit Nashville and the Cumberland overflowed its banks downtown, rising several blocks up Broadway. The entire basement of Big River was filled with water all the way up the spiral staircase that led down from the brewing room, flooding and floating all the serving tanks and making a general mess of the brewing systems. Big River was only closed for two weeks after the catastrophe, becoming one of the first restaurants downtown to recover from the event. Since all the beer in the tanks was ruined, the brewery shipped beer in from Chattanooga to satisfy customers who were curious to see what had changed downtown since the antediluvian days.

Later that year, New York–based private investment firm Centerbridge Capital Partners purchased majority stakes of both Rock Bottom Restaurants and Gordon Biersch Brewery Restaurant Group and renamed the new company Craftworks Restaurants & Breweries. Among the other properties within the larger portfolio of almost two hundred properties is Old Chicago Pizza and Taproom, a restaurant concept that features craft beers but without on-site brewing capabilities.

For almost three years, nothing changed at Big River in Nashville that would be visible to the consumer, but in April 2013, management announced the decision to change the name of the brewpub to the better-known Rock Bottom Restaurant and Brewery brand. They reasoned that since Nashville is such a popular tourist destination for visitors from all across the country, it was logical to present the name that they might be more familiar with.

Initially, some customers were startled by the substitution of their favorite old Big River beers with new Rock Bottom varieties, but each Rock Bottom location's brewer is encouraged to create his own recipes to include on the taps. The company is slowly moving away from corporate flagship beers to allow for more room on the taps for rotating selections. Since Rock Bottom only featured four national brands and added more tap handles after the transition, there is actually more room for experimentation and to feature local guest beers on draft.

Mortensen's personal tastes run toward IPAs and strong Belgian beers, and he enjoys being able to keep four or five special brews in the system at all times whenever there is tank space. Unusual for what you would expect out of a brewpub environment that tries to maximize throughput of that valuable tank space, Mortensen has been known to spend up to nine weeks lagering a maibock.

In a nod to the past, patrons can usually find at least one of the old Big River recipes on tap at the new Rock Bottom, usually the Southern Flyer and/or the Nashville Steamer. With more than seventy-five brewers corporation-wide within Craftworks, the brewpubs exchange award-winning and popular recipes between locations to allow more beer lovers to experience these brews and discover each brewer's individual take on the particular style.

Corporate mandates are more likely to take the form of fun contests in which each brewer is asked to come up with a unique summer seasonal featuring local honey or an annual Fire Chief Ale promotion where proceeds from a "brewer's choice" specialty brew benefit local firefighter charities. The advantage of the corporate environment is access to hard-to-source hops and specialty malts and the ability to trade ingredients between locations.

While the name over the front door may have changed from Big River to Rock Bottom, the people inside are still dedicated to creating a constantly evolving roster of inventive products for beer lovers from novices to connoisseurs.

PART II

MIDDLE TENNESSEE'S TWENTIETH-CENTURY CRAFT BEER RENAISSANCE

CHAPTER 8

YAZOO BREWING COMPANY

"MY HEAD'S IN MISSISSIPPI"

Nashville's brewpubs continued to be the primary options for local beer lovers to experience exotic styles of brews throughout the 1990s, but packaged craft beers from across the country were beginning to get a toehold in the market as Nashville beer distributors started to bring new options from craft brewers into bars and store shelves. As the populace began to acquire more educated palates and a thirst for better beer, a young entrepreneur from Mississippi had an inkling to enter the market in a new and different way.

Linus Hall started homebrewing with a kit he bought out of the back pages of *Rolling Stone* magazine while he was still a college student at the University of Virginia, where he studied mechanical engineering. A job as a process engineer at Bridgestone brought him to Nashville from his hometown of Vicksburg, and he almost immediately jumped into the local homebrewing community. As he honed his personal brewing style and developed recipes that impressed fellow brewers and friends, Hall began to daydream about the possibility of actually scaling up his hobby into a full-scale brewery.

The late '90s was a scary time to jump into the craft brewery scene, as some of the more successful operations around the country had been snapped up by larger players and almost immediately dropped out of favor with their previous fans who regarded them as sell-outs (which, literally, they had become). Undeterred, Hall kept discussing the idea with his wife, Lila. He says, "She finally got tired of me talking about it, so we committed to giving it a go. But we knew that we wanted to do it the right way." Less politely, she told him to do it or shut up about it and promised to do her part to help support them if he quit his tire engineering job.

Hall's corporate background had informed him in the business side of starting up a venture like this, and he knew exactly what he didn't know yet. To ensure that his finance and operations talents would be up to the task of running his own production business, Hall enrolled in Vanderbilt University's Executive MBA program so that he could study on nights and weekends while still maintaining his job at Bridgestone.

After receiving his EMBA in 2000, Hall undertook more technical studies from the American Brewers Guild in California, where he earned a craft brewing degree. He managed to attract the attention of noted brewer Garrett Oliver of Brooklyn Brewery and talked his way into an unpaid summer internship at the groundbreaking craft brewery. Hall's experiences at Brooklyn were instrumental in helping to develop both his brewing style and business acumen.

"Garrett taught me the 'four pint principle.' In order to make it as a small brewery, our beers had to be good enough for most people to want to drink four pints at a sitting. I felt like many folks in Nashville were looking for a local microbrewery to support, and we sought to brew clean flavorful beers with that were easy to drink and enjoy." That's a good thing, because Hall tried to get hired at Brooklyn Brewery but was politely encouraged to find his own way back in Nashville.

After returning to town, Hall sourced a used ten-barrel DME brewhouse and started looking for a space to put it. He discovered a space in Marathon Village, a North Nashville commercial development that had formerly housed the Marathon Motor Works a century before from 1907 to 1912. Actually, "development" is probably too kind of a word for the corner of the building that owner/entrepreneur Barry Walker showed to Hall as a possibility to rehab into his brewery space.

"Half the roof was caved in," Hall recalls. "All of the windows were boarded up, and there were thousands of pigeons living there. Barry could sense we were desperate and a little bit crazy, but we needed a space." Trying to preserve operating capital for the future, Hall bought most of his brewing equipment at auction and did most of the building renovations himself. Hall was determined to self-finance the venture so that he could keep control over business and creative operations without compounding the risk of an already precarious proposition. Plus, as Yazoo's chief beer evangelist and sales manager Neil McCormick likes to tell people, "All of our investors get in the same bed every night."

Yazoo's original location at the former Marathon Motor Works is now the home of Corsair Artisan Distillery.

Linus Hall and his wife, Lila, were the first two employees of Yazoo Brewing Company. The major shareholders still "get in the same bed every night."

It took about fourteen months to get it where he could actually occupy the space and start brewing at Marathon. One day during the rehab, Hall was standing precariously on the roof up to his ankles with dilapidated shingles when his phone rang with a call from Lila informing him that they were going to be parents. "That's how I can always tell how old the brewery is since it was born right about the same time as my first daughter."

Hall and his wife had already decided on a name for their venture, Yazoo, after the river that ran through his hometown of Vicksburg. Considering that his future distribution would include Memphis at the head of the Mississippi Delta and points south into the Magnolia State, it was a masterful marketing decision.

The brewery opened in October 2003 with a staff of three: Linus, Lila and his first brewer, Zach Henry. Lila designed the labels and helped out with any other necessary tasks, and Linus and Zach swapped out brewing shifts at least three times a day on their small brewhouse to keep the four fermenters full. Eventually, Yazoo would grow to twelve various-sized fermenters in the Marathon location.

Their initial offering was four core beers plus seasonal options. Hall personally called on local bars and restaurants selling kegs of Yazoo Pale Ale, Dos Perros, Spring Wheat and Onward Stout. "There were four brewpubs in town, but after Bohannon stopped brewing a few months after we opened, we were the only packaging brewer in the state." Self-distributing for the first year, Yazoo expanded to more than fifty retail outlets selling its beer on tap.

Hall never wanted to open a brewpub but made the decision to open a small taproom at the facility. He says, "We consider restaurants and bars to be our partners. We focus on making the beers and count on our partners to sell it. But the taproom offers an opportunity for us to interact with our ultimate customers." The cozy room became a popular gathering spot for beer nerds to focus on their favorite hobby. Unlike most Nashville bars, there were no televisions, no food and no live music. That last element offered an unexpected benefit, according to Hall. "In a musicians' town like Nashville where everybody respects the creative process, there are a lot of local musicians who tell me that they appreciate being able to just drink a beer without having to listen to someone else play and be all respectful about it."

After Yazoo's Hefeweizen won a gold medal at the 2004 Great American Beer Festival, it replaced Spring Wheat in the core offerings and was quickly joined by Sly Rye and the innovative Hop Project IPA. Every batch of Hop Project is brewed with a different combination of spicy hops, and recipes are never repeated after a batch is drunk up. Since labeling regulations would

Neil McCormick is Yazoo's "chief beer evangelist" and is a familiar face at beer festivals across the region.

have required approval for each individual batch if the information changed every time, every brewing of Hop Project is released in the same bottle design. Interested drinkers can cross-reference the bottled-on date with Yazoo's blog to find out the particulars of each recipe. Hall encourages homebrewers to take advantage of Hop Project to learn about the characteristics of some more exotic hops and experiment with them in their own small-batch recipes. Plus, the rotating roster of hops allows Yazoo to offer an IPA all year round, even during periods of difficult availability for certain hops.

With the disappearance of Market Street's bottle beer brands from the Nashville market, Hall seized the opportunity to take the next step down his original business plan into the world of packaging. Signing with local distributor Lipman to assist in getting placement in larger retail chains and for representation extending beyond the county line, Hall invested in a used six-head bottle filler/labeling line in 2005. Still financing his business strictly out of Yazoo's growing cash flow, Hall actually turned at first to volunteers to come into the brewery on weekends to help out with the bottling process in return for a few cases of beer. Despite a healthy crop of avid volunteers, a business advisor suggested that this process was a terrible insurance risk, so Hall hired more employees to help out in the brewery and work the packaging line.

Yazoo's sales growth far exceeded Hall's conservative business plan projections, and the brewery had quickly outgrown the space at Marathon. When the lease came due in 2010, Hall made the decision to purchase a building in Nashville's burgeoning Gulch neighborhood. The building that would house the new incarnation of Yazoo had previously been an air-conditioning supply company and before that the Tennessee Social Club, a gathering spot for "swingers." This seedy former operation did not deter Hall since he knew that the building would need a thorough sanitizing anyway to function as a brewery.

It was tough to move the entire operation, but he knew that Yazoo needed more space to continue to grow. Hall says, "I learned so much from the original Marathon brewery. For example, we had set it up so that when it was time to dump our used grain, it was all in the farthest corner from the door so we had to shut everything down and completely clear the floor to haul it all the way through the brewery. So we didn't make the same mistakes when we laid out the new brewery. We made brand-new mistakes."

Hall believes that the beer industry should be local and regional since it's difficult and expensive to ship unpasteurized product and keep it as cold as necessary. So he was and is committed to keeping a regional focus. But even limiting his reach to Tennessee and Mississippi, Hall knew he needed to build a much bigger brewing system to satisfy Yazoo's double-digit annual compounded growth.

The new brewhouse is a forty-barrel Newlands system with various tanks ranging from forty-barrel to two-hundred-barrel capacities. In total, the potential throughput of the brewery is about twenty-eight thousand barrels per year, making Yazoo the largest brewery in the state with the exception of the newly restarted Schlitz-Stroh-Coors commercial brewery in Memphis. With the recent craft brewing boom across the country, Hall discovered that the market for used equipment had dried up, so he got to build the system from the ground up.

Yazoo sold its original brewing system to Corsair Artisan Distillery, which moved like a hermit crab into the Marathon Village space and uses the brewhouse as the starting point for many of its award-winning craft spirits. Hall swapped out his first rickety bottling line for a much faster Italian-made filler/labeler. He considered adding a canning line instead but, after surveying customers, discovered there wasn't a clear preference

Huge tanks fill the brewery facility at Yazoo, but there is still room for cask-conditioned projects on the brewhouse floor.

for one packaging over the other. Hall personally believes that the seaming technology isn't quite there yet for cans but continues to keep an eye on the option as the packaging industry makes improvements.

An unexpected obstacle was getting zoning approval for Yazoo's grain silo on the corner of the building facing the busy Division Street. Hall had already experienced difficulties getting the OK to add a silo at the Marathon location in a little-traveled industrial neighborhood, so he looked for a creative solution.

In the end, he called it a sign structure as far as permitting was concerned and contracted local muralist Michael Cooper to paint a trompe l'oeil depiction of a giant fermentation tank complete with Yazoo-branded tap handles on each side. Hall added the extra expense of actually mixing copper in with the paint so that the silo, err…sign will develop a lovely patina as it ages over time.

The new taproom at Yazoo quickly became a popular gathering spot for the growing population of young urban residents of the fast-growing Gulch neighborhood. Still committed to concentrating on the brewing process and not wanting to siphon business from his bar and restaurant

The comfortable outdoor patio at Yazoo's taproom offers the chance to watch the world drive by in the Gulch while enjoying a pint of Yazoo brew.

partners, Hall only opens the taproom Wednesday through Saturday, though he could certainly fill the place all week long. Yazoo also hosts festivals and special brewing events at the facility, including a wildly popular Embrace the Funk Fest, featuring many examples of sour beers that Hall got excited about during a trip to Belgium. Kegs of sour beer are positioned around the brewery for visitors to sample until they run dry, upon which they have to rush to another corner to be surprised by what is being tapped next. Future plans for Yazoo include an off-site barrel storage area where the brewery can isolate the exotic natural yeast strains from the production area.

Hall had long wanted to experiment with high-gravity beers but was unable to acquire a distillery license to brew them. After years of talking to employees of the Alcoholic Beverage Commission, he finally found one with a sympathetic ear who helped him walk his way through the application process. The resulting product is a beer named Sue, brewed with a cherry wood–smoked malt that quickly became popular with Nashville drinkers, despite the fact that Tennessee's convoluted alcoholic beverage regulations did not allow him to serve it in his own taproom. Sue won a silver medal at the GABF and is available in retail locations that do have licenses to sell liquor by the drink.

Through the Tennessee Craft Brewers Guild, which Hall serves as president, Yazoo has been instrumental in lobbying efforts to address the state's craft beer tax rates that had been the highest in the nation. The group also managed to have the maximum threshold for low-gravity beers raised from 5 percent ABW (6.2 percent ABV) to 8 percent ABW (10.1 percent ABV), effective in 2017. While this is still low compared to some neighboring states, it does put Tennessee closer in line with other markets.

Yazoo also fills its tanks with the occasional contract project, including the return of Gerst Beer to Nashville production and a private label for its distributor Lipman that it calls Hap & Harry's. The brewery also collaborates with other brewers in town and even provided the wash for the award-winning Corsair's 100% Rye Whiskey, which surprised Hall since he considered it Yazoo's "worst mash ever." The sticky grains of the rye are notoriously difficult for brewers to work with, and the whole process was a real mess for everyone involved.

But Linus Hall has never been afraid of a challenge and almost always rises to the occasion. As the unquestioned Pied Piper of Nashville's craft beer community, Hall and his brewery continue to lead the whole industry. Future brewery expansions are in the works to meet the growing regional demand for Yazoo's products in more than six hundred retail locations, but Hall insists that the brewery will always operate as a local operation, just like it did when it had only three employees. Along with current head brewer Quinn Meneeley and a staff that has grown to fourteen full-time employees plus taproom workers, Hall is ready to lead Yazoo into the next decades.

CHAPTER 9

CALFKILLER BREWING COMPANY

"GOIN' UP THE COUNTRY"

After Bohannon ceased brewing kegs for distribution to bars and restaurants in 2004, Yazoo enjoyed exclusive status as the only Middle Tennessee brewery providing beer for restaurant and bar sales for six years. When another player entered the game in 2010, it arrived from an unexpected location.

Calfkiller Brewing Company is basically a two-man operation out of Sparta, Tennessee, the tiny county seat of White County on the Cumberland Plateau about an hour-and-a-half drive through the rolling hills east of Nashville. Brothers Dave and Don Sergio are the proprietors of Calfkiller, and you could say that they were born with beer in their blood. Hailing from southern Wisconsin, a state known for both the brewing and consumption of malt beverages, the brothers moved to Sparta in 1980 when their father fell in love with the town while helping to build a house for a friend. He became so enamored of the area that he asked his friend to let him know if any property nearby became available and soon moved his young family to a new homestead.

"Dad spent all his life in the construction business," shares Dave, "but the bureaucracy of dealing with the government on projects was killing him. When he came here, he fell in love with the plateau. It had a similar topography without all the taxes." The two Sergio brothers have lived in Sparta all of their lives since then with the exception of a few years in the late '90s when Don moved to Murfreesboro as a musician with the popular regional rock band the Features. When he eventually left the band, Don returned home and bought three acres of property in 2003.

Calfkiller Beer is proud to be "brewed in the backwoods of Sparta, TN."

Don and Dave had already started homebrewing in 2001 and took to the hobby with a maniacal interest. After two batches made from malt mixes, they quickly switched to using whole grains. Brewing constantly using a homemade ten-gallon system on weekends during breaks from their own construction jobs, the Sergios would often find themselves with thirty gallons of beer fermenting in carboy containers behind their couch. Although this pleased their thirsty friends, the other residents of the house were not quite as enthused, and Dave and Don began to eye the old cow stables on Don's new property as a potential site for their home brewery. Friends and family pitched in on the construction project to convert the dirt-floor building into at least a semblance of a professional workspace. At the time, their plan was to repurpose old military soup kettles as brewing equipment to increase their production capacity.

In 2006, the brothers decided that they could brew professionally to sell their beer at a few retail locations and at events and festivals while still keeping their regular day gigs, so they applied to the Sparta town council for a local beer permit. The three members of the council looked suspiciously at the young men as they showed a copy of the new legislation legalizing production brewing. Dave remembers, "We thought the laws seemed pretty straightforward to us that we could do this, but the council told us they wanted to consult the state attorney general." The AG issued an opinion that the Sergios' application was, of course, within the law. But the council members responded, "Well, that's just his opinion," and rejected the request again.

The Sergios had no choice but to sue the council and eventually won their case. They are especially proud of a photograph they took of the three stubborn councilmen signing the permit, like Lee surrendering at Appomattox. Next, they had to submit their plans to the feds for approval, and it occurred to them that this venture would have to be a full-time job to be worth all the time and effort.

If they were going to quit their construction jobs and make the leap into professional brewing, that stable would have to be a whole lot bigger than just a place to play around with a ten-gallon system. Using recycled and scavenged building materials, the Sergios added an extra story to the brewery building and laid it out with an eye toward installing somewhere between a three-barrel and a fifteen-barrel brewhouse. They planned ahead for drainage and cleanup by plumbing the entire building and lining the main room of the brewery with old donated tiles that a trained eye will recognize as coming from a 1970s-era McDonald's.

Scouring the Internet for used brewing equipment or anything that they could cobble into brewing equipment, the Sergios found a seven-barrel brew kettle in St. Charles, Louisiana, that they bought sight unseen. They drove down to pick up the JVNW kettle and brought it all the way back to Sparta. They now had the beginnings of a bona fide brewery!

Clever enough to add a garage door to the stable during renovations, they were free to move equipment in and out of the building as necessary, which is fortunate because some of the vessels fit between the ceiling and floor with scant inches to spare. After acquiring the brewhouse, they started collecting equipment for the rest of the brewery.

The area around Sparta used to be full of small dairy farmers, but with the advent of mega-dairies, no one had use for small milk storage tanks anymore. The brothers saw this as an opportunity and bought three old tanks to use as a mash tun and hot and cold liquor tanks for next to nothing. They then designed and built their own sparging system out of parts from an old washing machine.

Their fermenters came from an old brewery in New Mexico that had abandoned them years ago. "They never even cleaned them," Don recalls. "The tanks were full of fruit flies that had dined on the last batch of strawberry-kiwi wheat beer and died. It was nasty and took a lot of hard

The fermenters at Calfkiller, where the Sergio brothers spent hours cleaning the remnants of their previous life at a New Mexico brewery.

days of hose work to clean those out." The fermenters were lined with wood as an insulator, and the inventive brothers fashioned a chilling system for about $300 that was based on a home air-conditioning system to pump cold water through copper coils to cool down the tanks.

Finally, they built their own cold conditioning room adjacent to the brew room with five seven-barrel tanks and one fifteen-barrel tank that allows them to cold condition all of their ales for at least a week. When the construction dust finally settled, Calfkiller found itself with a four-vessel, seven-barrel brewing system with two seven-barrel fermenters and two fifteen-barrel fermenters. Blessed with excellent municipal water from the nearby Calfkiller River that gave its name to the brewery, the Sergios only have to run the water through a carbon filter to remove the chlorine before brewing.

The system is almost entirely manual, built like their original 10-gallon system, but scaled up to 220-gallon scale. Dave speaks to the simplicity of the design: "We mainly used late-1800s books to design our process. Gravity was the key to moving the beer around the system, and it's free." Indeed, there's just one simple light switch to turn a pump on and off to help move the liquid from tank to tank. "That pump was a big deal for us," Dave chuckles.

Dave Sergio viewed through the window into the tiny grain room at Calfkiller Brewing Company.

A small mill upstairs allows the Sergios to grind their grain on site but necessitates carrying nine fifty-five-pound bags of grain up a narrow flight of stairs for every brew. From their careers in construction, Don and Dave are not afraid of hard work, but they admit "that milling system might change. We're not getting any younger."

With only four employees and a chemical engineering intern from nearby Tennessee Tech University, Don and Dave do all of the brewing. A typical brew takes them about eight hours, and they brew four to five times per week. The rest of the time is spent cleaning the tanks and kegging the beer for distribution.

Since the brothers began homebrewing, they estimate that they have experimented with more than four hundred different recipes before repeating one, taking meticulous notes about the processes and results. Each batch was judged and named so that they could recall the details of the experience as opposed to trying to remember a batch number. The clever names of Calfkiller beers are one of their calling cards, usually derived from slang terms, local plants and animals, friends or experiences that occurred to them during brewing.

Memorable Calfkiller beer names include Brown Recluse, Wizard Sauce, Cluster F.U.C.T, Farmer Dave's White Winter Wizard Wit, Feature Creature, Deadhorse, Flat Tail Ale and Hacker's Harvest. Since the names weren't necessarily descriptive of the beer, this encouraged drinkers to experiment with new varieties without knowing what to expect from the glass.

This (lack of) naming convention worked well since the original distribution strategy was to try to get on taps at nearby drinking establishments, and the Sergio brothers knew that it would be difficult to displace the big boys from the limited tap space at boat docks, country dance halls and biker bars. Since these joints didn't have twenty different drafts like at a Nashville craft brew bar, the Sergios took samples to bar owners and asked for just one tap handle to be dedicated to Calfkiller. They then rotated through many of their recipes one keg at a time so that the locals could experience a wide range of their products.

Soon, they established their own small distribution company, Grassroots Distributing, to service the market in six surrounding counties where Nashville and Chattanooga beer companies didn't focus a lot of effort. By 2010, Calfkiller was in full production and distributing its rotating roster of beers.

Its core standard grades are Grassroots Ale, an American pale ale; J. Henry, an English dark mild ale; an American-style Classic Stout; and the cheekily named Sergio's Old Evil-Ass Devil Bullshit Ale, an American pale

Barrel-aging projects on the floor of the brewery at Calfkiller.

Although you can't buy beer at Calfkiller, you can pick up empty growlers, pint glasses, shirts and other swag.

wheat ale. Seasonal beers are an important part of its offering as well. From the brothers' experience in the construction business, it was always a big deal to receive some sort of bonus around the holidays, so Christmas Bonus became the name of the brewery's special winter offering, which can feature seasonal flavorings like apple, cinnamon or even pine needles. Their spring/summer seasonal is an amber ale that they call Scorned Hooker. During the fall and winter, she morphs into a Scorched Hooker, the darker sister in the form of a black IPA.

The Sergios also like to experiment with barrel-aged beers, including Evil Dead, aged in a Corsair Distillery Quinoa whiskey barrel, and a hot pepper beer that they conditioned in a barrel that they had already used five times. The mad scientist brothers added four scorpion peppers to the brewing process, only after sampling the smallest sliver of what is considered to be one of the hottest peppers on the planet. Once their tears subsided, they decided to throw three more habaneros into the keg for good measure before serving the infernal brew.

Another fun project for Calfkiller is playing around with smoked grains. Dave explains, "2013 was the year of smoke around here. We had ordered a ten-pound bag of smoked peated grain to experiment with, and the company accidentally sent us a fifty-five-pound sack. So we added it to everything." The smoked malt comes from Simpson's in Scotland and is the same grain that is used in the finest single-malt scotch whiskies. The resulting peat-smoked Belgian Ale is called Smokey Treat and is a popular treat indeed when it comes around in the Calfkiller brewing rotation. The brewery also collaborated with Yazoo to produce the Beacon, a special unfiltered brew made with oak-smoked wheat malt, local Tennessee honey and in-house Calfkiller-roasted coffee. Proceeds from the Beacon helped to fund the effort to lower Tennessee's high craft beer tax.

Thanks to another of Tennessee's odd alcohol regulations, the Sergios can't legally sell any of their beers in the small taproom attached to the brewery, since White County does not have the minimum of seventy-five thousand residents. But they do attract between fifty and sixty beer enthusiasts from all over the world to make the trek to Sparta to tour the brewery on Saturdays, sample beers and purchase T-shirts and other swag. Their visitors are enthused by the brothers' stories and dedication to their craft, and the Sergios are always appreciative of the company.

That desire to interact with their customers is also why the Sergios don't participate in many of the numerous beer festivals across the region unless they can actually attend in person. Rather than just sending a keg to be poured by a volunteer for thirsty festival attendees, Dave prefers to take that role himself. He says, "It's about making friends and sharing what's in our brains. We have so many options to bring our favorite weird stuff to festivals, especially since we can't actually sell our barrel-aged high grav products."

The first festival they ever exhibited at was the first festival that they had ever attended, the inaugural East Nashville Beer Festival in April 2011. While they enjoy traveling to meet their fans, every time one or both of the brothers leave the brewery, production pretty much shuts down. Dave has a plan, though. "We'd like to make Sparta more of a destination. We have plans to build a taproom with a restaurant attached plus canoe, kayak and inner tube rentals so that folks could float from the brewery to downtown Sparta, and we could pick them up and bring them home again."

With ninety distribution outlets spread between Nashville, the Cumberland Plateau and Chattanooga, Calfkiller is pretty much maxed out on its current production capacity with a waiting list for its beers. It might still be able to grow a little bit more in the old cow stable, but Dave worries, "It's a hard process. We're working on steps to make it easier for the two of us to make all this beer."

If the Sergio brothers do expand Calfkiller Brewing Company or realize their dream of a taproom/restaurant, it's a pretty safe bet that if they build it, beer lovers will come.

CHAPTER 10

COOL SPRINGS BREWERY

"SUBURBAN LEGENDS"

When Chris Hartland retired in 2008 after a career in the British military, he and his wife, Jane, decided to move to America to open a business venture. "It could have been anything," Jane recalls, "a laundromat or a liquor store." At the time, Chris was a fairly loyal Stella Artois drinker, so craft beers weren't exactly on his radar. Searching potential business opportunities, the Hartlands discovered a pizza parlor named Guido's in Franklin, Tennessee, and decided to buy it and convert it to a brewpub.

Work visa in hand, the couple moved to the States with their two young children in tow after the purchase closed in September 2008, not exactly a boom period in the American economy. They hired the aptly named Mike Kraft as their first brewer and set about purchasing the equipment to move into the former pizza joint to make it a proper pub.

Settling on a seven-barrel brewhouse with a two-vessel system, along with five seven-barrel fermenters and bright tanks, the newly named Cool Springs Brewery served its first beer in October 2009. Patrons could watch the entire brewing process conducted in the cramped space right inside the restaurant's front door and enjoy fresh, cold beers directly from serving tanks or kegs behind the convivial bar.

Kraft's first craft was named Franklin's First in honor of its status of being the first beer brewed commercially in Williamson County. A German-style kölsch, the crisp light beer is made from a combination of two row pale malt, Munich malt and wheat malt flavored with German hops and is still on the regular menu at Cool Springs.

Above: Cool Springs Brewery is located in a nondescript strip mall in Franklin, Tennessee.

Left: The brewhouse at Cool Springs is located right inside the front door in full view of bar patrons enjoying their craft brews.

Other standards that can usually be found on tap at Cool Springs are Fatback Amber, a German altbier with color, aroma and flavors contributed by caramel malt, and the brewery's number-one seller, Pecker Wrecker IPA, a dry-hopped India Pale Ale with a firm, hoppy bitterness and elements of floral and citrus characteristics added from the hops.

After Kraft left to pursue an opportunity at another brewery opening up in Franklin in 2012, the Hartlands sought out a new brewmaster. Half a country away in Boulder, Colorado, a young brewer named Derrick Morse was looking for used tanks on the ProBrewer website when he encountered the want ad from Cool Springs. Conveniently, Morse's parents lived in Franklin, but he couldn't believe that there was a brewery anywhere near the hotbed of suburban rest that is Cool Springs. Inconveniently, Morse's wife was nine and a half months pregnant at the time and scheduled for induction two days after Derrick discovered the ad. He actually conducted his phone interview with the Hartlands while she was in labor and started his new job in Tennessee just six weeks later.

After a career as a marketing director for a software company in Boulder, Morse had been downsized in 2008 and decided to pursue a career in professional brewing after years as a homebrewer. He says, "I was pissed off that I wasn't any better at homebrewing, so I committed to learning the craft from the floor up." This turned out to be a literal commitment as his first job at Twisted Pine Brewing Company was mopping floors and cleaning kegs. He also offered marketing advice to the company and moved quickly up the ranks thanks to his production management skills.

Morse gained a reputation as a very creative brewer at Twisted Pine, and his West Bound Braggot ale/mead hybrid brewed with orange blossom honey, pungent Citra hops, Tasmanian pepper berries and Buddha's Hand, a fragrant citrus fruit, won a gold medal at the Great American Beer Festival before he left the brewery in 2012. As part of his negotiations with the Hartlands, Morse requested creative freedom to spread his wings and play with new recipes in addition to the old standard recipes. The Hartlands were happy to oblige.

Morse's experience in project management served him well as he moved from the brewer of a large production brewer to the small seven-barrel brewpub system at Cool Springs. "Brewmasters have to be good managers. It's like a weird version of that old video game Tetris as we move all the parts together to keep the tanks full and still constantly experiment with new recipes. We make a lot with a very little system, but it also allows for lots of fun things since we aren't saddled with a thirty-barrel system," he says.

While Morse is responsible for most of the creativity in the brewhouse, the management team works together to come up with the often-puerile names for new batches, occasionally allowing fans to vote for their favorite choice on Facebook. Cheeky brews like Titches Wit, Bulging Kilt, CircumSaison, Franklin's Twigs n' Berries and Kilt Lifter may sound like a tittering schoolboy's playground joke, but they are deadly serious brews.

For example, Titches Wit is a summer seasonal brewed in the style of three of Morse's favorite Belgian witbiers. Redolent with orange peel and coriander, this clean Belgian is full of citrus and malty character. Cool Springs Brewery takes full advantage of the restaurant's attached commercial kitchen with several other beers. The Twigs n' Berries is made with blackberries that the staff handpicked at a nearby farm and then processed in the restaurant's kitchen. Cool Springs tries to use some sort of local ingredient in at least half of its beers, from tea to spices, berries and honey. The smell of roasting pumpkins or spices being ground in the kitchen for use in the brewery certainly grabs the attention of patrons who know they will unfortunately have to wait until the brewing process is finished for their ultimate gratification.

The hardworking Morse is a huge coffee fan to keep his energy level up and, truth be told, would probably choose java over beer if forced to pick. Instead, Morse has combined his two loves with Early Riser, an American Sweet Stout made with a custom blend of Peruvian and Ethiopian beans that have been roasted to Cool Springs Brewery's specifications by local purveyor Roast, Inc. A popular Coconut Stout featured more than twenty-five pounds of toasted coconut shavings blended with a rich Belgian candy syrup to create a beer that reminded some drinkers of an Almond Joy candy bar.

Often Cool Springs will experiment with small pilot batches to get the opinions of its loyal legions of fans before ramping up production. Thanks to already having a liquor license, it was fairly easy for the brewery to receive a distillery permit to produce high-gravity beers. A popular experiment was its Mango IPA, a 6.2 percent ABV beer made with four different malts, 2 row, Crystal 60, Crystal 30 and White Wheat malt, and then hopped with Centennial, Cascade and Falconers Flight. The resulting beer is an interesting West Coast–style IPA with plenty of mango, pine and grapefruit notes on the long finish.

Not only does Morse experiment with many exotic hops and malts, but he is also a strong believer in polycultural yeast brewing with five different strains of in-house yeasts banked. While some breweries fear introducing more than one strain of yeast into their production, often rightfully,

The bar at Cool Springs serves the brewery's craft beers from serving tanks located right behind the bartenders.

Cool Springs enjoys experimenting with sour beers, albeit at a separate warehouse facility. Morse is particularly excited about a saison injected with *Brettanomyces* spores that he has aged for more than a year in oak barrels from the nearby Arrington Estates winery. He has also aged other batches of beer in whiskey barrels from Prichards, Collier and McKeel, Elijah Craig, Jack Daniel's and Corsair.

In addition to encouraging a loyal following of beer drinkers through a Beer Club that rewards frequent visitors with perks like their own steins and discounts for the Top 25 customers who receive 22 oz. pours for the pint price, Cool Springs Brewery also works closely with the homebrewing community. As part of his desire to give back to the same sort of folks who might someday follow his path into the profession, Morse offers an internship program for young brewers to learn the ropes. He also works with homebrew clubs like the Mid-State Brew Crew and Music City Brewers. In fact, Cool Springs' assistant brewer Jonathan Adams is a past president of the MCB.

Cool Springs sponsors a Pro/Am brewing competition that is open to all comers. A panel of four judges including Morse picks a winner from more than one hundred entrants. The beers are judged "bracket-style" against one another like the NCAA hoops tournament until a final winner is determined. The first year's winner was a maple/pecan porter that the homebrewer was allowed to brew with Morse in a seven-barrel batch to be served at Cool Springs and entered into the GABF.

The brewery also maintains a frequently updated blog where Morse and the Hartlands share information about the brewpub and the brewer gives descriptions of current releases and advice to homebrewers. The sense of community created by the brewery's continual outreach efforts has paid off for the business. Jane states, "We've gained sales consistently from both the food and the beer, but the beer keeps people coming back. It's great that we're gaining a reputation as a proper brewery." Cool Springs has earned kudos for its pub food as well, introducing an authentic fish-and-chips dish brought over from England by Jane's father, who ran a "chippy" in Great Britain.

The latest big development at Cool Springs Brewery has been the leap into packaging. In addition to growler fills, the Hartlands and Morse had always wanted to bottle their beers for a wider distribution. In early 2014, Cool Springs partnered with local beer distributor Ajax Turner to release a series of four of its most popular beers in twenty-two-ounce bomber bottles.

The process was a grassroots effort with the staff designing and building their own four-head bottle filler in the Hartlands' garage capable of putting out twenty cases per hour. A local tattoo artist created a bold bottle design to feature the new CSB brand, and a crew of staff, interns and volunteers worked weekends to apply the individual labels to each bottle to differentiate between the four releases.

The first offering of beers was sent to more than thirty liquor stores with particular focus on high gravs. The four beers were: Hop Brutality, a 9.8 percent ABV Imperial IPA; CircumSaison, an 8.2 percent ABV Imperial Saison; Brussel's Muscles, a Belgian strong ale coming in at a whopping 10.1 percent ABV; and the popular West Coast IPA Pecker Wrecker, brewed at 7.2 percent ABV. Early sales figures have been promising, and Cool Springs Brewery hopes to expand into a new production facility sometime soon, in addition to maintaining the brewpub. Plans are for a 30-barrel brewhouse with 120-barrel fermenters.

Future plans might include introducing the brewery's products in cans and starting to mill its own grains on site. Whatever the future brings, you know that the Hartlands and Morse will continue to innovate within the brewpub. "The stuff we're doing now is calculus," Morse promises. "Wait until we get into quantum physics!"

CHAPTER 11

JACKALOPE BREWING COMPANY

"I AM WOMAN, HEAR ME ROAR"

Bailey Spaulding, the co-founder along with Robyn Virball of Jackalope Brewing Company, grew up in Vermont. Despite the fact that her home state has the highest number of breweries per capita in the country, it never occurred to Spaulding to open her own brewery. She says, "I loved beer, but I never thought real people like me could brew it." She also thought that the rest of the country was blessed with her region's wide variety of craft beers: "I just assumed that the beer you drink is what everybody drinks."

Spaulding met Virball in September 2002 in the famous Scottish golfing village of St. Andrews, where Bailey was doing a semester abroad and Robyn was completing her undergraduate degree on the way to a master's degree in English. In 2006, Spaulding moved to Nashville to enroll in law school at Vanderbilt University. During her 1L year, she got into the hobby of homebrewing and started to reconsider her career options. Having a background in biological anthropology where she conducted noninvasive studies in cognitive evolution, this was more of a logical leap than most might imagine.

"Basically, I studied monkeys on an island off of Puerto Rico," she shares. "My experience in science taught me to conduct experiments with the desire of repeatable results, so I just considered brewing to be a similar undertaking." She tried to start a homebrewing club at Vandy Law School, but found the market underserved in terms of craft brew enthusiasts.

"I loved Nashville and knew it would be a great place to start a business because the community is so supportive," she says. After graduating with her law degree in 2009, Spaulding called her old friend Virball, who had been toiling along in a corporate marketing career in Boston. "Robyn jumped at the chance to move to Nashville, and our skill sets seemed like they would complement each other nicely."

Bailey took a job working for the Land Trust of Middle Tennessee, even growing some hops at the organization's historic Glen Leven Estates farm on Franklin Road near downtown. The two women spent the next few years developing their first three core recipes, brewing half-barrel batches on a small SabCo system and throwing parties where their friends from school and the craft brew community could vote and comment on their favorites. All the while, Spaulding and Virball were working on a business plan to open their own full-scale production brewery.

They optimistically expected that it would take about six months to open, but it took more than double that amount of time before they could begin brewing. After taking on some investment from friends and family, Spaulding and Virball still maintained the majority stakes in their company, which they named Jackalope after the mythical rabbit/antelope hybrid that Bailey admits she long ago thought was real. She was once given a T-shirt with a picture of a jackalope on the front and the inspirational slogan "Believe in Yourself!" Cheesy as that might sound, it has become the unofficial motto of the company: "Believe in yourself. Believe in good beer."

Bailey and Robyn spent part of the summer of 2010 visiting Lazy Magnolia Brewing Company in Kiln, Mississippi, to learn more about the business and processes behind craft brewing from owners Mark and Leslie Henderson. When they returned, they were ready for Jackalope to find a permanent hutch.

The two partners discovered a building on Eighth Avenue near the edge of the Gulch and SoBro neighborhoods, right around the corner from Yazoo's new digs. It was formerly the Kirkland Flooring and Paint building with the eventual brewhouse occupying the space where the previous tenant stored carpet rolls and the showroom turning into a taproom.

The building had the bare minimums for a brewery's needs: a thick concrete pad for a floor, high ceilings and a loading dock to receive grain and ship beer. The added bonus was that it was near the center of Nashville's downtown, and foot traffic was quickly growing through the neighborhood, a development that could be very beneficial to the young brewery's success. "I was worried that Linus would think that we were moving in on Yazoo's territory," remembers Spaulding, "but he's been so helpful in our work to establish a new Brewery District here in the Gulch."

The signs indicating the front door of the taproom at Jackalope Brewing Company feature the mythical rabbit/antelope hybrid that inspired the name of the brewery.

Bailey and Robyn signed the lease on the building in December 2010 and began to design the brewhouse themselves, since there was nobody in town who specialized in that sort of engineering. While they waited for equipment and licensing approval, the duo continued to brew on their small SabCo and eventually opened their taproom on May 21, 2011, serving beers only from the small pilot system. Even with the taproom only open for limited hours on Fridays, Bailey found herself brewing seven days a week to keep up with the demand plus obligations to visit various beer festivals.

Jackalope took on its first intern in Steven Wright, who joined the crew during the summer of 2011 to help out with the brewing. His dedication paid off in the form of an official partnership with Spaulding and Virball and the eventual title of head brewer.

The initial offering at Jackalope was three core beers. The first was named after Davy Crockett's wife, Thunder Ann. An American pale ale made with Chinook and Cascade hops and then dry-hopped with a heaping helping of Citra, Thunder Ann quickly became a very popular example of West Coast–style APA. The second opening beer was inspired by the maple trees of Spaulding's native home state. Bearwalker Maple Brown Ale is actually infused with pure maple syrup during the conditioning process and benefits nicely from roasted chocolate malt and a heavy hand of hops to create a complex beer. The third core beer from Spaulding and Virball's initial experiments was Rompo Red Rye Ale, their take on an Irish red. Jackalope adds flaked rye to the mash to contribute a little twist to the usual UK hops and caramel malts of a traditional Irish red ale. The namesake of Rompo is a little twisted, too, referring to another mythical beast with the head of a rabbit, the ears of a human, the front arms of a badger and the rear legs of a bear.

Eventually Jackalope would add a fourth core beer with Leghorn Rye India Pale Ale, a complex version of an IPA with three different types of rye and five separate additions of hops varieties during the brewing process. In addition to the core four, Jackalope keeps rotating specials and seasonals on its taps, including some lighter-drinking varieties like the very popular Love Bird, a Hefeweizen brewed with large amounts of wheat, strawberries and raspberries. The brewery tries to introduce a rotating special every four to six weeks for the two taps in addition to the four core beers, often partnering with other Nashville businesses.

The brewery bragged that its Jackalope Snowman Stout was "abominably good," thanks to the addition of mocha flavors from local Bongo Java coffee. Jackalope Tannakin was another version of a mocha stout brewed in partnership with Corsair Artisan Distillery, which donated one of its Quinoa Whiskey barrels in which to age the finished beer. The name of the beer comes from the story of Mistress Tannakin Skinker, a lovely woman who was cursed to have the head of a pig. True to the beer's inspiration, Tannakin is infused with bacon and an extra kick of vanilla courtesy of local cocoa nibs. Released in very limited amounts in bomber bottles, Tannakin is a very sought-after beer whenever Mistress Skinker makes an appearance.

After months of brewing on what Bailey describes as a "just in time system" where the taproom ran out of beer every Friday at 7:00 p.m., Jackalope finally received delivery of its fifteen-barrel brewhouse system that had been manufactured by Pacific Brewing Systems. "It arrived four months late," remembers Spaulding, "and it was a little bit of a nightmare. There were no manuals. It was miswired, and it took seven months to install. But we were already paying rent, so we just had to keep plugging away."

The first batch from the new system came off the line on December 1, 2011. Production ramped up over the next couple months as Jackalope began distributing kegs to bars at the beginning of 2012. Within six months, the initial sixty-barrel fermenter was operating at capacity, and a second

Once the Jackalope crew members figured out the wiring for their Pacific Brewing Systems brewhouse, they were finally able to ramp up production for the taproom.

was added with another on the way. With four times the capacity of the brewhouse, each tank takes twenty-eight hours of brewing to fill, but the increase in efficiency has been critical to Jackalope's growth.

Spaulding already has an eye on further expansion, saying, "We've got room for at least a few more years here. It seemed like such a huge space at the time, but we have to plan three to five years out. We've added two assistant brewers, Sally Cooper and Will Hadley, who started out as interns."

A major addition has already taken place in the form of packaging. In late 2013, Jackalope partnered with Moe and Carl Oelker's portable canning company named Toucan. Based out of Chattanooga and Bowling Green, the Oelkers bring their Wild Goose Canning Technologies MC-250 four-head filling system in a twenty-foot box truck to the brewery to package more than ten thousand cans in a run that are then delivered to Jackalope's distributor Bounty Beverage for shipment to stores and bars. The brewery is currently canning Thunder Ann with plans to expand its packaged offerings in the near future, including seasonal releases like Love Bird. "We'd love to brew more Love Bird," says Spaulding, "but with more than two hundred pounds of fruit in each batch, it gets kind of expensive."

Pallets of Jackalope Thunder Ann ready for distribution, courtesy of Toucan Portable Canning Company.

Recovered barn wood and paper lanterns create a peaceful ambiance in the Jackalope taproom.

The taproom is still only open sixteen hours per week, but a partnership with Zollie Wilson to open a coffee shop in the taproom space has allowed for better utilization of the space and more foot traffic to the brewery. ZolliKoffee also offers baked goods that help to fuel the hardworking employees of the brewery. The taproom only offers limited food options when open, but at least once a week it partners with Kathleen Cotter and her gourmet cheese shop the Bloomy Rind to present platters of elegant *fromages* to accompany Jackalope's brews.

Now distributed in more than two hundred outlets from Clarksville to Chattanooga, Spaulding is particularly proud of one of the brewery's first placements, thanks to Austin Ray, a local craft beer advocate and restaurateur: "When we went into M.L. Rose, Austin kicked Miller Lite off the taps. That made us feel really good!"

Ever the scientist, Spaulding plans to continue with the spirit of experimentation at Jackalope. She says, "We always want to keep trying new things. But most of all, we like to have fun with what we do, and we hope our customers will have fun too."

Chapter 12

TURTLE ANARCHY BREWING COMPANY

"Happy Together"

Similar to its neighbors to the east at Calfkiller, Turtle Anarchy Brewing Company is also a family affair, this time with the three brothers of the Kamp family. The brewery was the brainchild of the eldest brother, Mark. He moved from Cape Cod to Nashville in 2005 to attend Belmont University and study the music business. As a junior, a friend talked him into trying homebrewing using a kit, and Mark discovered he really enjoyed it.

His record label management classes convinced him that he really didn't want to go into the industry as a profession, but he plugged on, graduating with a triple major in music business, marketing and finance in 2010. Kamp's educational background did prepare him for a career in the beer biz, so he began to accelerate his brewing experiments and work on a business plan.

His younger brothers, Andrew and David, had also moved to Tennessee from Massachusetts to study at Middle Tennessee State University in Murfreesboro. The Kamps brewed five-gallon batches together every Saturday, learning the tricks of the trade and developing their own personal brewing style. Turtle Anarchy still has its SabCo Brew Magic pilot brewing system at its modern new facility, but it's not a museum piece or landmark like the garages where Apple or Hewlett-Packard were founded. The Kamps still use their original system for trial recipes or special small-batch products.

As Mark worked on the formal business plan, he was simultaneously seeking investors to back the new venture. Eventually, the decision was

Turtle Anarchy's Mark Kamp holding one of the novel mini-kegs that can be personalized as gifts.

made to keep the ownership completely within the family. By early 2011, all three brothers had moved to Nashville to commit to the business. An early advisor was Jason McMurray, the managing director of Lipman, who would eventually become the brewery's distributor. As the distributor of Yazoo beer as well, McMurray suggested that Turtle Anarchy seek to produce complementary styles of beers instead of trying to go into direct competition with another brewery with a big head start. Bailey Spaulding and Robyn Virball of Jackalope were about a year ahead of the Kamps in their journey to beer entrepreneurship and were very helpful with advice for the brothers.

The pilot brewery system at Turtle Anarchy is still used for small batches of specialty brews.

The original brewhouse at Turtle Anarchy will be replaced by a larger facility in West Nashville.

The name of the brewery demonstrates Turtle Anarchy's methodical approach to the craft brew market. Mark explains, "We consider Turtle Anarchy to be synonymous with 'slow revolution,' and that's our ultimate goal. We want to win drinkers over to craft beer, specifically ours, one pint at a time."

Late in 2011, the Kamps found a brand-new unoccupied warehouse building in a new commercial development on the outskirts of Franklin. As the first tenants, the Turtle Anarchy team was able to build out the building to its specifications. Taking over three bays of the flexible space, the Kamps designed their brewhouse with advice from some of their other mentors in town. However, since most warehouse lessees prefer and expect level floors in their buildings, there was a considerable amount of work to be done to trench and slope the floor to facilitate the sort of drainage required by a production brewery.

Once the building was prepared, Turtle Anarchy took delivery of its tanks and brewhouse in February 2012. The system was fabricated by Premier Stainless Systems out of California and featured a fifteen-barrel two-vessel brewhouse, hot and cold liquor tanks, four thirty-barrel fermenters and one thirty-barrel bright tank. The first head brewer at Turtle Anarchy was Mike Kraft, who had moved over from Cool Springs Brewery, and Mark and Mike went through training together on the new brewing system.

The fledgling brewery received its official Brewer's Notice from the federal government in May 2012, so it was free to begin legally brewing on the new system. Harkening back to the Kamps' homebrewing experience, Mark described the styles of beer that they wanted to produce to Kraft, who then developed the specific recipes at a fifteen-barrel scale. The first beer that they brewed together on June 13 was a citrus-forward rye IPA that they named Another Way to Rye.

Excited to play with their new toy, Kraft and the Kamps brewed three other batches of what would become Turtle Anarchy's initial core offering that same week. In addition to the rye IPA, Portly Stout, a golden ale named Aurumglass and At Wits End, a Belgian witbier, soon followed Another Way to Rye into the kegs in Turtle Anarchy's walk-in cooler.

The initial plan was to open a small taproom at the front of the brewery three days per week for four hours a day, but one important landmark had to be achieved: the youngest brother, David, had to turn twenty-one so he could work there. That momentous birthday arrived on July 2, 2012, and Turtle Anarchy welcomed the public to its taproom three days later for a busy July Fourth weekend.

The taproom did not and still doesn't serve food, but patrons are welcome to bring their own nourishment with them or order from several delivery services in the neighborhood—not that it mattered much at first, since the thirsty guests were busy discovering the newest brews in town at the taproom and various beer festivals. For the first forty-five days, Turtle Anarchy self-distributed its beer to restaurants and bars, but state regulations do not allow breweries to distribute outside of their home county. Even with this limitation, Turtle Anarchy found its way onto several taps within the first month before Lipman came on board to facilitate broader distribution.

In addition to their core flagship brews, the Kamps were dedicated to producing small-batch specials and five "rotators," seasonal recipes that occupy two- to three-month blocks in the brewing schedule. A classic German helles lager named Infidelis Helles was released in December 2012 and quickly supplanted Aurumglass as one of Turtle Anarchy's three core beers, along with the rye and the stout.

Portly Stout became one of the most popular beers at the taproom, where guests quickly drank the kegs dry. It also serves as the palette for Turtle Anarchy's series of experimental infusions that it labels Fifty Shades of Black. A fairly straightforward example of a stout, Portly Stout takes on the flavors of spices well, and the brewers can remove a valve stem from the conditioning tanks or kegs to drop a mesh bag full of toasted coconut or coffee from local roaster Bongo Java or habanero into the beer to steep like a tea bag. Each small batch of the Fifty Shades series receives its own special name with the three previously mentioned versions called Down With the Coconut, None More Black and Damnation, respectively.

Other notable special brews include a prototypical brown ale named How Now Brown Cow, Hail the Pale APA, Pretty Fly for a Weiss Guy, an American amber called Scarlet Harlot and 1864, a smoked porter commemorating the Battle of Franklin. These beers are brewed in larger batches for distribution through Lipman, but other smaller batches are produced as one-offs for taproom use or beer festival specials. Examples of these microbrews are Crystal Heff, More than Meets the Rye and Smoke & Mirrors, a version of Turtle Anarchy's stout steeped with dried chipotle peppers and coarsely ground cinnamon.

Opening with just two full-time employees and some part-time help, Turtle Anarchy added Dan Dutcher as assistant brewer under Kraft in September 2013 after he had worked as an intern since January of that year. In March 2014, Dutcher replaced Kraft as brewmaster after Kraft left for other opportunities.

After a little more than a year in their original facility, the Kamps began to plan for expansion, and that meant searching for new space to brew bigger batches to keep up with growing demand. With distribution in more than 150 accounts in the Nashville, Knoxville and Chattanooga markets, Turtle

David Kamp of Turtle Anarchy demonstrates the special resealable keg-tapping system that the brewery employs for its infused beers.

Anarchy plans to move to a new twenty-five-thousand-square-foot brewing facility in West Nashville. While it will still maintain its taproom and use the brewing space for small batches and cask conditioning, the brewery has a new thirty-barrel three-vessel system on order for the new facility.

While there are no plans for a public-facing presence at the new brewery in the old Dixie Wire warehouse at Sixtieth and California in Nashville's Nations neighborhood, it will be a major development for the city's beer-drinking population. Entering into a new joint venture named Southern Anarchy, Mark Kamp will manage a suite of auxiliary services for local brewers including keg leasing, a canning line and a bottling line. Southern Anarchy will have the capability to pick up brewed beer in tanker trucks for packaging and deliver the finished products directly to distributors.

Turtle Anarchy's fifteen-barrel system is now on the market, but the brewery already has plans to fill up the new bigger brewhouse with some contract brewing as well as expansion of its own brands into cans and into new markets. Considering the Kamps' business acumen and the fact that the three founding brothers of Turtle Anarchy are still in their twenties, there is plenty of time for them to expand their empire considerably.

CHAPTER 13

FAT BOTTOM BREWING

"YOU MAKE THE ROCKING WORLD GO 'ROUND"

Fat Bottom Brewing founder and head brewer Ben Bredesen has deep roots in the Nashville community. The son of the city's former mayor and governor of Tennessee, Ben's last name is an instant door-opener in town, but the young entrepreneur definitely stands on his own two feet. After graduating from Brown with a degree in computer science in 2002, Bredesen returned to Nashville to enter the healthcare technology industry as a director of software development before eventually progressing to vice-president of marketing at Qualifacts.

Along the way, Bredesen discovered an interest in and a talent for homebrewing, a hobby that he had first tried while an undergraduate in Providence. After one brew from a kit, Bredesen immediately progressed to his own whole grain recipes. In 2010, he got serious about brewing with friends on five-gallon and ten-gallon systems, and he enjoyed playing around with various styles of beer.

Bredesen had long yearned to open his own business and started considering various ideas in 2010. He says, "At first, I thought about a brewpub, but I knew I wanted to get into production brewing since there was so much more growth potential selling outside of just one building." By early 2011, Bredesen heard that a friend was looking at a space in Nashville's Germantown neighborhood and kicked himself that somebody had beaten him to the punch.

Buckling down on the search for a brewing site, Ben started to look around his home neighborhood of East Nashville. When developer Dan Heller

The William Gerst Brewing Company was one of the largest production facilities in the South. At its peak, it produced over 200,000 barrels per year. *Courtesy of Scott Mertie from the collection of the Gerst Haus.*

The present-day site of the old Gerst brewery is an abandoned lot at the corner of Sixth Avenue South and Mulberry Street.

Above: The logo for Gerst featured a script "G" for the owner wrapped around a dove as a symbol of purity. *Courtesy of Scott Mertie.*

Left: Gerst produced a popular series of advertising lithographs featuring beautiful women and only a small mention of the brewery's name. *Courtesy of Scott Mertie from the collection of the Gerst Haus.*

Kent Taylor (left) and Stephanie Weins (right), the founders of Blackstone Brewing Company. *Courtesy of Blackstone Brewing Company.*

Head brewer Karen Lassiter (left) and assistant brewer Jimmy Randall (right), of Boscos.

Head brewer Brad Mortensen of Rock Bottom Restaurant and Brewery.

Linus Hall of Yazoo Brewing Company is the acknowledged godfather of many new Nashville craft brewers. *Photo by Adam Jones, courtesy of Yazoo Brewing Company.*

Left: Yazoo's infamous grain silo, camouflaged as a sign outside the brewery.

Below: The taproom at Yazoo is a popular gathering spot in the Gulch for craft beer lovers from all over town.

Left: Hops growing on the outdoor patio at Yazoo's taproom.

Below: Yazoo's Comac bottling line is capable of putting out 350 cases per day with only two operators.

The brew crew at Jackalope Brewing Company. *From left to right*: Will Hadley, Robyn Virball, Bailey Spaulding, Sally Cooper and Steve Wright.

Don (left) and Dave (right) Sergio of Calfkiller Brewing Company with their tools of the trade (and a beer, of course).

The brewery at Calfkiller is a converted cow stable that the Sergio brothers renovated with scraps from construction jobs.

Cool Springs Brewery released several of its most popular beers in bomber bottles in 2014.

The taproom at Turtle Anarchy is worth the trip to the hidden industrial strip park in Franklin, if only to try its limited-release special brews.

Fat Bottom Brewing's owner/brewmaster, Ben Bredesen, stands behind the bar of his convivial taproom.

Left: The taproom at Fat Bottom is a destination for families, cyclists looking to rehydrate after an urban ride or anyone in search of a fine hamburger.

Below: The logos for Fat Bottom's cans were designed by Anderson Design to harken back to the voluptuous pinup girls of an earlier age.

Above: The massive brew room at Mayday Brewery features tanks named after the staff's musical heroes and guitar gods that passed too soon.

Left: Ozzy Nelson, the owner of Mayday Brewery, is "the man" and a popular tour guide for Saturday visitors. Come prepared to have a good time!

Ken Rebman built almost every element of his Czann's Brewing Company facility himself, down to the drywall in the taproom.

John Owen (left) and Carl Meier (right) of Black Abbey Brewing Company catch up on some inspirational reading.

Even the parking signs at Black Abbey play off of the Belgian monastery theme of the brewery.

Corsair Artisan Distillery contributes its used barrels to many breweries around town to experiment with barrel-aged brews. This barrel is at Black Abbey.

Garr Schwartz (left) and Christian Spears of Tennessee Brew Works stand proudly in front of their revolutionary Meura mash filtration system.

Part of the taproom at Tennessee Brew Works offers a front-row seat to view the modern brewery at work.

The sampler at Tennessee Brew Works showcases the wide variety of beer styles produced at the brewery.

Lines of thirsty Nashvillians queue up to attend the East Nashville Beer Festival organized by Matt Leff of Rhizome Productions.

The Filling Station offers many local and regional craft beers for growler fills or by the bottle at their two locations.

The M.L. Rose Craft Beer and Burgers location in West Nashville is the brainchild of Austin Ray, an early advocate of Nashville craft brewers, who compete for tap space at the bar.

The industrial-chic design of Fat Bottom's facility reminds visitors of the building's former incarnation as the Fluffo Mattress factory.

showed him the old Fluffo Mattress Factory on Main Street, Bredesen knew he'd found his space and signed a lease in October 2011. While the building wasn't ideal for a brewery—with ceilings that are just barely tall enough and needing a new concrete slab to be poured and trenched to support the heavy tanks and facilitate drainage—Bredesen loved the 5,500-square-foot space. He says, "I wanted an accessible area that felt personal, where people could be able to reach out an almost touch the brewery. However, we still have to deal with people stopping in looking to buy a mattress every now and then."

Another brewery venture, Broadcast Brewing Company, signed a lease two months after Bredesen. The plan was for the two breweries to share a courtyard and taproom between their respective production facilities. Unfortunately, Broadcast never opened, so Fat Bottom remains the only brewery in the hip East Nashville section of town.

With a location secured, the studious Bredesen researched more than twenty potential manufacturers for his brewing system. Relying on his management experience, he sourced his equipment just like any other industrial purchase through a series of phone calls to vendors. In the end, he selected California's Premier Stainless Systems for his fifteen-barrel brewhouse to pair with four

Visitors to the Fat Bottom Brewing taproom walk right past the brewhouse where the beers they are about to enjoy are produced.

fifteen-barrel fermentation tanks plus fifteen-barrel and thirty-barrel bright tanks. Eventually, an additional ninety barrels of tanks would be added in May 2013 with even more on order to keep up with demand.

The build-out and brewing system installation took place during the first quarter of 2012. Bredesen turned to Powell Design Studio as an architect and contractor to create an efficient workspace that transitioned into the warm gathering spot of the taproom and courtyard patio. Bredesen has a young daughter, and it was critical to him that Fat Bottom was a kid-friendly environment for families to enjoy food and drink together. He says, "It was really important that it be a place that I could hang out at."

With live music on Thursdays and a food menu of small bites and upscale tavern food including burgers, salads and vegetarian options, Fat Bottom has quickly established itself as the sort of neighborhood hang that Bredesen was hoping for. While the pinup-style drawings created by Anderson Design Group to delineate each of Fat Bottom's brands might not be completely family friendly to the most prudish of consumers, they were very well thought out, along with the name of the brewery.

Powell Design employed barn wood and retro lighting fixtures to create a comfortable environment for the Fat Bottom taproom.

Clever single men know to visit the patio outside of Fat Bottom when the adjacent hot yoga studio lets its students out of class to enjoy a cooling pint.

"I started out with a list of a couple hundred potential names," Bredesen recalls. "I didn't want the name of the brewery to be based in our geography, because I always had goals of being a national player. 'Fat Ass Brewing' made people laugh and was certainly memorable, but it was just too over the top. Fat Bottom was still memorable and travels well. Most importantly, I knew we had to have both good liquid and good branding."

When Bredesen finally opened the brewery and taproom on August 17, 2012, he was all by himself in the production room with just a little bit of help on days when the beer garden was open. Premier Stainless sent an engineer to help set up the equipment and train Ben, but after he left, it became a solo operation. Even now, Bredesen still does the bulk of the brewing on the primarily manual system by himself, often brewing four to five times per week, including some double batches, to fill the tanks with Fat Bottom's most popular beers.

The brewery opened with three out of the five planned core beers on tap, all of which were named after women and featured lovely ladies as label models. Black Betty India Dark Ale benefits from a combination of German malt and American hops to create a smoky beer with floral notes. Ginger American Wheat Ale is based on a Belgian krystalweizen, or clear wheat ale, and is brewed with a high proportion of wheat plus a dose of fresh ginger during the brewing process. This crisp ale quickly became a popular summer seasonal for Fat Bottom. The third opening beer was an American red ale named Ruby. Hoppy without being overly bitter, Ruby came roaring out of the gates as Fat Bottom's bestseller, a designation that it still holds.

Two other flagship brews followed quickly behind the original three with a full-bodied oatmeal stout named Bertha and Java Jane Coffee Porter. Fellow East Nashville entrepreneur and bean roaster Drew's Brews provided the cold-brewed coffee that contributes intense flavors to this malty, sweet-finishing beer. Similar to the evolution of Ginger, Java Jane earned the spot as Fat Bottom's cold weather seasonal stalwart.

Outside of the five standards, Bredesen brews other special beers for the taproom and small releases from the ten-gallon pilot brewing system to be featured on Wednesdays. Fat Bottom's Knockout IPA started out as one of these specials and quickly grew into the brewery's number-two seller for its wholesaler DET Distributing. Ida, a Belgian golden ale, combines Pilsener malt with delicate Goldings hops to create a light-bodied ale that has grown into the most popular beer at the taproom. A small batch Saison Noir is another favorite during the spring while autumn brings Scottish ales aged in used barrels from Buffalo Trace or Belle Meade Bourbon.

After four months of self-distribution, Bredesen signed on with DET as the brewery's distributor in Middle Tennessee. "I wanted to be a brewer," states Breseden pragmatically. "I had no desire to be in the distribution and logistics business." In addition to developing a few local accounts at neighboring bars and restaurants, Bredesen had an eye on packaging his products for retail sales. Canning offered the opportunity to expand Fat Bottom's geographic reach, so Bredesen jumped at the chance to buy a used canning line from Brewery Vivant in Grand Rapids, Michigan. After training on the machine during a canning run in Michigan, he had it shipped to Tennessee to offer Ruby and Knockout in cans.

The taproom still provides the majority of the revenue for Fat Bottom, but future plans revolve around moving into a new production facility. Like Turtle Anarchy, Fat Bottom wants to maintain its current taproom and move the brewhouse to a new larger location. Bredesen says, "We're definitely looking to stay in East Nashville, because that's important to the identity of the brewery. We hope to expand the dining room and event space here at Fluffo, but the new facility will be strictly functional."

With 150 barrels of current fermenting tank space, production capacity would max out at around 1,100 barrels per year, and Bredesen has much loftier goals than that. Already distributed from Jackson, Tennessee, to Chattanooga, Fat Bottom aims for a smart expansion rollout. According to Bredesen, "In smaller markets, maybe we'll only release one or two beers at first. I just want to introduce customers to our balanced style of beers that have character without going over the top."

"Smart," "balance" and "character" are all words that could be used to describe the crazy-smart but humble Bredesen. His goal of becoming a national player could definitely become a reality.

CHAPTER 14

MAYDAY BREWERY

"CALL IT HEAVY METAL"

Mayday Brewery founder Ozzy Nelson has always wanted to be "the man." But at his day gig as an internal auditor for the huge Hospital Corporation of America, he knew it would be difficult to ever become more than "a man." Originally from Daytona Beach, Nelson moved to Tennessee at the age of twelve and graduated from Smyrna High School in 1983. Growing up, he was convinced that the reason why his father had children was to have someone to change the channel on the television for him and fetch him a beer from the refrigerator, so his love of beer comes from an honest place.

He started brewing in his garage from malt extracts and added hops in 1993, but the thought of opening a brewery never occurred to him until 2009, when he made the decision to look for investors in the production brewery of his dreams. Without the benefit of family money to depend on, Ozzy developed a business plan and went on the hunt for money. His grass-roots efforts paid off with enough capital to start the process, but he remains the major investor in Mayday.

The name of the brewery also comes from his father, who would refer to any snafu as a "mayday." One day while Ozzy was brewing in his garage, he left the kettle unattended for a moment when his wife, Pamela, entered the house to announce, "We have a mayday. The wort is boiling over." And the brand was born.

Nelson spent 2009–2012 planning his brewery and brewing the same four beers over and over in five-gallon batches to nail down the recipes and demo them for feedback from friends and potential investors. He also consulted a few other brewery owners for advice, and the one thing they all said was that they wished they had built bigger brewhouses. So he went in search of a big-boy system.

He knew he wanted to buy from a North American manufacturer and got estimates from several companies. In the end, he felt like he clicked with the Canadians at DME Brewing from Prince Edward Island. He ordered a thirty-barrel two-vessel brewhouse, four thirty-barrel fermenting tanks and two thirty-barrel bright tanks to start out with. Ever the gambler, Ozzy hadn't nailed down a ship-to address for his new equipment at the time of purchase, but he quickly struck a deal for twelve thousand square feet in a former textile factory in Murfreesboro.

He closed on the building in April 2012 and began the process of building out the space for the massive brewery; two walk-in coolers to store kegs; a taproom with multiple rooms, patios and decks for socializing and live music; and a notable lack of any office space whatsoever. "I don't need an office," states Nelson. "I want to be where the people are and the action is all the time." Mayday's small staff did much of the renovation work themselves, which allowed them to add their own special touches, like a secret room where special invited guests can enjoy a shot of rum and some animal crackers with brewery staff. Mismatched furnishings and cheesecake paintings of busty beauties were acquired through Craigslist and yard sales to decorate the walls of the brewery and taproom.

Even more important than finalizing the décor of the new facility was finding someone to help Ozzy run the brewery. Nick "Wiz" Wisniewski came on board as brewer with the experience of working on a thirty-barrel brew system at Two Brothers Brewing Company in Chicago and musical talent on the guitar and bass, which came in handy as a member of the Mayday staff rock-and-roll band known as the Yeasty Boyz.

Music is very important to almost every aspect of Mayday. Live bands are frequently featured in the taproom or on a makeshift stage on the brewery's loading dock. One stipulation is that all the bands must play original music, with the exception of the Yeasty Boyz, who consider themselves "the best Black Sabbath tribute band this side of Patterson Avenue." With Wiz on bass, co-brewer John Overby on drums (with the occasional heavy metal xylophone solo), self-dubbed Minister of Beervangelism Charles Nelson contributing all three guitar chords that he knows loudly and in random order and Ozzy yodeling or going off on spoken-word poetry rants on the virtues of craft beer, a performance by the Boyz is not to be missed.

Beer lovers travel from Nashville to Murfreesboro to experience the fun atmosphere at Mayday Brewery's taproom and fill up their growlers.

Mayday Brewery has multiple indoor and outdoor spaces to enjoy a pint of beer and listen to live music.

The infamous Yeasty Boyz Mayday band features brewery employees playing entertaining versions of their favorite heavy metal classics.

A drum kit illuminated by disco lights sits among the rafters of the brewery with a female mannequin seated on the drummer's throne. Even the fermentation tanks are named after some of Mayday's favorite rock guitarists who died too young: Stevie Ray, Jimi and Randy Rhoads.

On Ozzy's birthday, November 30, 2012, Mayday officially opened and invited the public to join in the party. Nelson's very personal approach to sales really began to reap benefits once he had the opportunity to make new fans for his beers. In addition to working the taproom with his wife and a few other part-time employees, Ozzy often leads entertaining tours of the facility in which guests learn about the fun personality of Mayday and sample its four core beers.

Although Ozzy doesn't have a lot of hands-on involvement with the brewing process at Mayday, no question is off-limits during these half-hour brewery tours. Ozzy relates, "I tell all of my tours that I am an open book. You can ask me anything that you like, and I will give you the very best honest answer that I can. I also say that they can take any picture they would like on the tour. If you would like one of our recipes, take a picture with your phone of one of the clipboards on those tanks, take it home, scale it down to

Oh sure, there's a mannequin playing drums in the rafters at Mayday Brewery.

your system and brew it yourself." He prides himself on learning the name of every participant on his tours, unless they get really big. Then he just memorizes the women's names.

The brewery opened with four core beers that are still in production. Their flagship Evil Octopus gets its name from the eight separate additions of hops during the brewing process, one for each leg of the aquatic cephalopod. An American black ale that's as dark as squid ink, Evil Octopus is sharply floral with bitter hop notes and a creamy texture. Boro Blonde is an American blonde ale reminiscent of a German kölsch-style ale. Glacier, Crystal and New Zealand hops contribute fruity character to Mayday's most sessionable beer. Angry Redhead is a malty American amber beer with a spicy nose thanks to Chinook hops. The final core beer at Mayday is Velvet Hustle, a balanced APA made with Victory and Honey malts plus a shot of American hops for floral and earthy notes.

Seasonal small batch offerings include John's Brown, a typical brown ale; Talk to the Hand Coffee Stout made with coffee locally roasted at Nuance Coffee & Tea; and Mayday Soul, a schwarzbier dark lager that is too opaque for light to pass through.

Although Ozzy had hoped to be canning his beers within the first year, sales were still entirely through kegs and growler fills at the taproom as of 2014. On an average week, the taproom accounts for about 20 percent of Mayday's sales during its operating hours Thursday through Saturday. The rest of the brewery's production passes through taps at more than 120 venues in Middle Tennessee. Ozzy makes frequent appearances at tap takeovers and other events with his distributor Lipman to take advantage of the opportunity to meet his customers face-to-face and inform them about the Mayday experience.

To accommodate the growing demand, Mayday added two more ninety-barrel fermenters and a ninety-barrel bright tank in July 2013 and has taken on a contract brewing position with Jubilee to produce its Randy's IPA. Although Wiz returned to Chicago to brew at Off Color Brewing, Mayday planned ahead by hiring John Overby away from his job brewing for Popcorn Sutton to serve as co-brewer and eventually replace Wisniewski.

At Mayday Brewery, the tongue-in-cheek corporate manifesto is "We try hard not to suck!" Judging by the brewery's growth and acceptance at so many drinking establishments in Middle Tennessee, it is staying true to that motto.

Chapter 15

CZANN'S BREWING COMPANY

"FRENCH KISSING IN THE USA"

In a town full of musicians, Ken Rebman is his own one-man band. At his brewery, Czann's (pronounced "zons"), Ken is the brewer, salesman, janitor and construction foreman and would be chief bottle washer if his beers came in bottles. He does wash the kegs, though.

Located in a nondescript bay of an industrial building on Lea Street near the new Music City Center, Czann's is a hidden gem in Nashville's young revitalized Brewery District. Rebman moved to Nashville from Huntsville, Alabama, in 1996 for a job opportunity as a controller for a local business. The next year, Ken brewed his first batch of homebrew from a beginner's kit. He soon became fascinated by his new hobby and got involved with the Music City Brewers club. Taking advantage of his background in finance, Rebman served as treasurer for the group.

Brewing with friends and fellow club members, Rebman experimented with many styles of ales, progressing from using malt mixes to whole grains. When he bought a new house with a basement for his home brewery, he switched to 100 percent whole grain and eventually began to mill on his own instead of depending on local brewer supply store All Seasons to grind his grain for him. "I actually bought the house because it had a basement," Ken recalls. "I didn't really care about the part of the house above ground because I figured I could fix all that, but I couldn't dig a basement."

In his new subterranean laboratory, Rebman brewed batches as big as twenty gallons, progressing from using carboys as fermenters to steel kegs to finally building his own conical fermenter. In 2003, he decided to get serious about his hobby as a business and left his career in accounting.

Enrolling in Belmont University's MBA program, he drafted a business plan for a brewery as a class project. He was still undecided whether his venture would be a brewpub or a production brewery, but he was determined that malt and hops would be his future.

After receiving his MBA, he began to search for a potential location and source equipment for his brewery. The process was slow as the real estate market was very unstable in the uncertain times of the late 2000s, and deals kept falling through. Since Rebman was the only investor in his potential business, he had to be smart with his money and do everything that he could on the cheap.

In late 2011, Rebman saw a listing for the equipment of a Rock Bottom Brewery brewpub system for sale at a bargain-basement price. He flew to see the system the day after he discovered it and wrote a deposit check on the spot. Now the proud owner of a compact eight-barrel three-vessel brewhouse from JVNW with four double-batch sixteen-barrel fermenters and a similar-sized conditioning and carbonation tank, Rebman really needed a building to house his equipment.

The answer to the problem came in the form of a three-thousand-square-foot building tucked on a side street between Nashville's wide avenues in the SoBro neighborhood. Rebman says, "It wasn't much to see, but it had everything I needed to brew: four walls, a dock door and high ceilings." Of course, there was no running water and the electrical system had to be completely rewired to handle the load of a production brewery, but Rebman was undeterred.

Despite having no formal experience as a building contractor, Rebman took on as much of the refurbishing as he legally could: "If codes would permit me, I'd do it myself." While his DIY attitude might have slowed down his official opening, it did save him a tank load of money from his personal savings.

In October 2011, his new brewing system arrived on the back of a flatbed truck and was forklifted through the dock door into the middle of the still-bare brewery space. As a brewpub system, it was fortunately quite compact. "It is definitely old school," Rebman relates. "Thanks to the direct-fire system, it's a lot like my homebrewing system, just bigger."

During the year and a half that he spent building out his new location, Rebman continued to brew at home and started to showcase his recipes at local festivals. Friends who had enjoyed his wares from his past twenty-gallon batches understood what he was trying to do and helped spread the word

The compact brewhouse at Czann's Brewing Company came from a closed Rock Bottom brewpub facility in Texas.

and build buzz about the impending arrival of the new brewery, which now had a name.

Despite inferences that "Czann's" is a nod to the famous French impressionist Cézanne or a goof on the Belgian farmhouse beer style of saison, the truth behind the name is much more personal. It's actually a combination of his mother's last name, Czora, with Ken's last name of Rebman. While it might be difficult to Google, it is a name that is both memorable and meaningful.

Czann's officially received its Certificate of Occupancy at the end of 2012 and started brewing in March 2013. Ever self-reliant, Rebman chose to handle his own distribution in-house, limiting his sales to Davidson County. He still handles all sales calls himself and enjoys sampling and explaining his beer to bar and restaurant owners and their customers.

His first sale was in April 2013 to local craft beer cheerleader Will Newman for his new growler fill shop in 12 South. The Filling Station has been an early supporter of many local breweries, and Newman was pleased to be the first to offer Czann's Pale Ale. Rebman was certainly happy to be on tap there after his long path to opening.

Czann's uses an inventive system of plastic kegs that are less expensive and lighter than traditional steel containers.

The single batch of Pale Ale that Rebman brewed was very well received, and he soon found himself on taps all around town. The recipe had been perfected five years earlier in his basement and scaled up nicely to the 250-gallon batch. "I thought it would be a refreshing option for people who don't like bitter pale ales," brags Rebman. "I try to make it well-balanced and drinkable, but I laugh when I hear people call it a session beer. I don't know about you, but I can't drink too many 5.25 percent ABV beers in a session."

Growth was slow but steady for the first few months while Rebman ramped up his production and finally hired Chad Hintz as an assistant. This fit exactly within Czann's conservative business plan. "Too many people try to choose how much money they want to make and then build a plan backwards from there. I wanted to build my business the right way," advises Rebman.

After three months of peddling his Pale, Rebman introduced a new beer to his portfolio, Czann's Blonde Ale. Lower in alcohol than the Pale Ale at 4.25 percent, Rebman's version is different from most blonde beers. To create this crisp, drinkable ale, Rebman employs five different malts and a light hand with the hops to produce a complex flavor profile that pairs very well with food, especially pizza. He says, "Pizza joints love the Blonde, and it represented 55 percent of our sales during that first summer of 2013." Also developed during his homebrewing days, Czann's Blonde was intended to be a "gateway beer" to help convert Bud Light and other national brand drinkers to the wonderful world of craft brews.

After the successful rollouts of his two core brands, Rebman started to brew single batches of special recipes to fill half of his sixteen-barrel fermenters. Czann's first seasonal was Pumpkin Ale made with real pumpkin and flavored with cloves, nutmeg and cinnamon sticks. It was quickly followed with Belgian Blonde and a surprisingly light and chocolaty Oatmeal Stout.

Rebman's most popular specialty brew has been Czann's IPA. Not as hoppy and citrusy as some West Coast–style IPAs, it fits within the balanced style of malt and hops that the brewer prefers. Never one to seek out extremes, Rebman brewed his IPA at about 6 percent ABV and fifty-two International Bittering Units (IBU). Unfiltered to allow some of the character of the yeast to remain in the glass, Czann's IPA is far from a hop bomb.

Unfortunately, as a small start-up brewery, Czann's does not have long-term hops contracts or ready access to the more exotic ingredients. He notes, "I knew that people loved the IPA, but I couldn't go right back to brewing it after the first release was gone." By March 2014, he gave in to the public clamor and officially named the IPA as Czann's third core beer.

The small taproom at Czann's has quickly gained a reputation as a downtown gathering location for a quick pint or two after work or on a weekend.

The next step in Czann's growth was the opening of an eight-hundred-square-foot taproom at the facility in June 2014. True to his nature, Rebman built out the space himself, and the industrial/warehouse vibe of the tasting room with exposed trusses is appropriate for the neighborhood and allowed Ken to not worry as much about finishing it with fine fixtures. He did soften up the space a bit by decorating the walls with framed grain bags from France that were actually used to transport Czann's raw materials to the brewery.

The chance to sell his product on site contributes nicely to Czann's bottom line, although Rebman continues to grow his presence at more than twenty venues in Nashville. Currently brewing for twelve hours straight once or twice per week and working every day on sales and construction, Rebman hopes to spend more time in the brewery. He says, "We've got plenty of room to grow in this facility through sales since we're only using about a quarter of the capacity. It's still pretty much a manual system where I mash in with a paddle. I touch every grain that goes into the beer, and that's what I enjoy."

Apparently, the fans of Czann's enjoy it, too.

Chapter 16

BLACK ABBEY
BREWING COMPANY

"PAINT IT BLACK"

After most of a decade of eight breweries bootstrapping themselves into existence in Middle Tennessee primarily using their own savings to build new facilities, the investment landscape in Nashville began to change in the early part of the 2010s. Carl Meier, an experienced homebrewer with a background in banking, was the perfect entrepreneur to seize on this opportune climate to open the Black Abbey Brewing Company, a modern facility located in an industrial park in Berry Hill near 100 Oaks.

Along with partners John Owen and Mike Edgeworth, Meier has created a facility that has room to grow and legions of thirsty followers who crave their primarily Belgian-style brews. Meier's love of beer and interest in brewing fermented while he was in college. In 1993, while taking what he figured would be an easy class titled Introduction to Wine and Spirits, his Cornell University classroom was visited by a guest lecturer to explain the wide world of beer to the neophytes. Previously a Schaefer and Carling Black Label sort of beer drinker, Meier was not familiar with the name of the authority. He thought Michael Jackson was the King of Pop, not the British authority who would open Meier's eyes and taste buds to the amazing global styles of beer that had never made it into his dorm mini-fridge.

Unfortunately, Meier's college budget did not measure up to his newly developed champagne tastes, so he decided to try homebrewing with a college buddy. An investment in Charlie Papazian's homebrewing bible, *The Complete Joy of Homebrewing*, furthered the future change in course of his life's work.

But first, he had to earn some money, so Meier toiled in nonprofit management and commercial banking for more than a decade after graduation. Work brought him from New York to Nashville in 1999, and his wife suggested that he join the Music City Brewers (MCB) club to make some new like-minded friends. While he met many great brewers in the MCB, several of whom would go on to open their own commercial breweries in town, eventually the group meetings at Boscos became too smoky, and Meier found himself spending more time brewing in unofficial meetings in the garages of friends. (Like most Nashville restaurants, Boscos eventually went smoke-free in 2007.)

As a member of the Antioch Sud Suckers, Carl made the acquaintance of another talented brewer named John Owen. The pair clicked in terms of beer styles and temperament and started an unofficial brewing partnership. A 2009 visit to Stone Brewing Co. introduced Meier to the brewery's barrel-aged version of its Arrogant Bastard beer. The professional brewers at Stone had good things to say about some of Carl's homebrew that he had brought along with him, and he was so taken by the new style of oaky beer that he decided to brew up a batch himself to enter in the National Homebrew Competition.

It took ten brewing sessions on their five-gallon system for Meier and Owen to fill a fifty-five-gallon Jack Daniel's barrel. They aged their beer more than one hundred days and shipped samples off to the competition. To their surprise, their brew garnered the highest score in their region and won a silver medal as the second best in the country in the category. Suddenly, that business plan that Meier and Owen had started idly working on in 2008 seemed much closer to a real possibility.

Mike Edgeworth, a local neurologist, came on board as the third co-founder and secretary of the new entity. His job was to stay on top of the economics of the new venture while Meier would concentrate on marketing and sales and Owen would serve as head brewer. Or, as Meier describes it, "John is the gas. I'm the brake, and Mike handles the steering."

Together, the trio worked on their business plan on Thursday nights while maintaining their day jobs. Black Abbey's coming-out party was at the first Nashville Winter Warmer beer festival on December 11, 2011. Hoping to introduce Nashville beer lovers to the potential of the brewery, Meier and Owen brewed up multiple batches on their home system to share with festival attendees.

That same month, Black Abbey began its capital raise in earnest, closing the first round of funding in November 2012. Meier remembers, "With the uncertainty of the financial markets, lots of liquid cash had been pulled out of the market. Nashville's growth was attractive to potential investors, and beer has a cool factor and charisma. We wanted to build an advisory structure of people who were willing to work on our behalf, not just pitch in money. You can't start a business focusing on the exit strategy; the only way to continue growing is to make great beer." It's easy to spot the investors enjoying a glass of Black Abbey in the tasting room, since only owners are allowed to drink from the special steins stored behind the bar.

With start-up money in place, Black Abbey ordered its brewing equipment immediately and ramped up the search for a brewery. "We had a list of attributes that we wanted in our new space: a strong concrete slab, high ceilings, a dock door, big water pipes and easy access to the sewer system," remembers Meier. "But with all of us holding down full-time jobs, it was tough to spend lots of time looking at prospective properties." Fortunately, the first building they looked at in their preferred neighborhood of Berry Hill was perfect for their needs, and they signed a lease in January 2013. Three months later they were ready to start construction.

The building had previously housed a bookbindery before the current owner bought it at auction and scraped it down to the slab. He then constructed a spec building on top of the old floor and sat on it waiting for the perfect tenant. "It was as if he designed the building to be a brewery," marvels Meier. "It was easy to lay out the work process area and didn't require a lot of demolition. We built up a brewing deck with fresh concrete and trenched out the drain lines so that all the wash-down water would run to one place. Taking advice from Linus at Yazoo, we floated the drains over the trenches."

Indeed, many brewers were quite helpful to Black Abbey in its start-up efforts. Local businessmen like Linus Hall of Yazoo and Mark Kamp from Turtle Anarchy offered advice, along with Jason Malone of Birmingham's Good People Brewing and Tim Herzog of Flying Bison in Buffalo. Kent Taylor of Blackstone sent his maintenance manager over to the construction site about every ten days, "just to make sure we weren't screwing anything up majorly," remembers Meier. "We certainly appreciated the culture of cooperation that we discovered among the Nashville brewing community."

The build-out took less than six months, and Black Abbey brewed its first batch of beer in August 2013. The brewing equipment was ordered new from California's Premier Stainless and consisted of a 20-barrel brewhouse with three 40-barrel fermenters and a 40-barrel bright tank. The works are steam-powered by a boiler purchased from Allied Boiler Supply in Murfreesboro.

Black Abbey Brewing Company's John Owen works on top of the Premier Stainless twenty-barrel brewhouse.

Capacity for the system is about 2,500–3,000 barrels per year, but plans to expand fermenting capabilities are already in place for late 2014.

Owen and Meier's brewing style trends toward Belgian beers, but they don't feel constrained by any particular flavor profiles. Meier explains, "Beer competitions are structured like dog shows where each breed is judged against specific style guidelines. We found that our favorite beers didn't always receive the highest scores. We preferred beers that were delicious but didn't necessarily conform to the standards of the style. We like to brew beer that we like to drink, plain and simple."

The Belgian style is ideal for such freethinkers, as it allows for much flexibility and creativity. Trappist monks brewed with whatever ingredients were readily available and allowed their personal taste preferences to shine through, unlike the more regimented German brewers and their strict *Reinheitsgebot* purity laws.

The brew crew members at Black Abbey like to tinker with their recipes and consciously work with two different yeast strains despite the fact that this complicates production. "Our American Chico yeast that we use in the APA is well-behaved," shares Meier. "But the Belgian yeast demands to be at the forefront of flavor."

When their first full trial batch was in the bright tanks, Carl (the brakes) thought it was too bitter to release. John (the accelerator) felt it was technically fine and wanted to keg it and ship it immediately. Mike (the steering wheel) was the tiebreaker and voted to let their baby loose into the world, where it was immediately well received. Plus, they were in a race with Tennessee Brew Works (opening at almost the exact same time) to get their first product into market.

They pulled the trigger and shipped the beer to M.L. Rose and the Taste of Tennessee Beer Festival that was going on as part of the Tennessee State Fair. "John was putting the kegs in the van for delivery," recalls Meier. "He was yelling at me, 'What's the name of the damn beer so I can write it on the keg collar?' So I sat in the office with the Bible open and started looking for a name."

As a testament to the difficult decision to release the beer, they named it Jude after a story of their inspirational historical figure, Martin Luther. When he was a monk, Luther lobbied for certain books to be excluded from the Bible, and the book of Jude was one of his suggested omissions because it referred to the Apocrypha. Despite Luther's protestations, Jude was included, and just like Jude, the beer was released.

The initial lineup consisted of three beers that Black Abbey calls the "canon," although it readily admits that the canon may change aim at some point in the future. The first three releases consisted of two Belgians and one American-style beer.

The first of the Belgians was a blonde ale called the Rose. The lightest regular offering at the brewery, the Rose is made with wheat malt. With an ABV of 5.8 percent, taproom patrons can enjoy more than one stem of the Rose. The second Belgian goes by the appellation of the Special. A yeasty amber ale meant to be consumed with food, the Special is a mild brown beer with sweet malt notes.

Patriotically named, the American stock pale ale goes by the name of the Champion. A traditional monastic-style ale with a frothy head, the Champion features backbone courtesy of English and smoked malts.

The intention at Black Abbey was never to limit itself to just the canon, though. Special beers started to arrive in quick progression, and the brewery's goal is to always have six to seven beers in the market at all times, requiring a deft management of its limited fermentation tanks. Meier comments, "As homebrewers, that's what we did. We still experiment with our old five-gallon fermenters to stay close to our homebrewing roots."

Black Abbey usually has several barrel-aging projects going at any one time, featuring casks from different distilleries and a variety of beer styles.

Notable special brews include POTUS 44, a robust smoked porter that was initially intended to be a winter seasonal as part of a Presidential Series of beers. Meier jokes, "We named it after Obama because it was liberally infused with Kenyan and Hawaiian coffee, and it has a little bit of smokiness that just won't quit." But when Nashville residents got hold of the beer brewed with a special batch of coffee that local roaster Frothy Monkey had chosen specifically to emphasize the coffee aromatics while minimizing the innate acids and oils, they just couldn't get enough of it. Black Abbey extended POTUS 44 into a second and third term, although a Berliner-style beer based on JFK's visit to the Berlin Wall is still planned for the future, as well as POTUS 40 to commemorate Ronald Reagan's admonition to "tear down this wall!" now that Tennessee laws have changed to allow liquor retailers to remove the physical walls between the spirits sides and beer sides of their stores.

Other small-batch taproom specials feature the creative use of barrel-aging techniques with casks from Tennessee distilleries Corsair, Collier and McKeel and George Dickel, plus Kentucky's Buffalo Trace adding its oaky goodness to some of Black Abbey's standard brews. The brewery has also

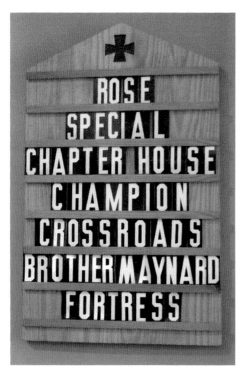

Above: The taproom at Black Abbey is referred to as Fellowship Hall and encourages socializing thanks to narrow communal tables.

Left: Never afraid to feature the brewery's monastic theme, the daily lineup of beers at Black Abbey is displayed on a hymnal board.

partnered with local confectioner Bang Candy Co. to use its sweet syrups to prime kegs before adding its beers, allowing the contents to steep and acquire fascinating characteristics.

In 2014, rather than bemoaning Punxsutawney Phil's annual declaration of more bad weather if the fickle rodent spots his shadow on February 2, Black Abbey instead chose to emphasize "8 More Beers of Winter" on Groundhog Day by creating sort of an internal tap takeover of all the taps in its own Fellowship Hall with unique barrel-aged versions of its favorite brews, including limited editions of some past favorites that their fans had thought were long ago drunk dry.

Events like this are a major reason why Fellowship Hall, Black Abbey's name for its taproom, has become so popular so quickly. Open to the brewery in full view of production, Fellowship Hall opened on September 26, 2013, just as soon as Black Abbey had brewed enough different beers to stock all of its taps.

Owen and Meier take advantage of the opportunity to meet their fans and talk about Black Abbey's philosophy or just about anything else that might be of interest. With five handmade farm tables designed to encourage conviviality, Fellowship Hall is opened for limited hours Thursday through Saturday and is located just a few minutes off the Armory Drive exit on Interstate 65.

With Black Abbey beer already available at more than 125 venues across Tennessee, the owners of the brewery don't look to move too large a percentage of their product through the taps at Fellowship Hall, lest they find themselves in competition with their primary customers. However, they will never pass up an opportunity to interact with fans of their beer because they realize that all of their future growth will result from converting new drinkers, one at a time, to the legion of Black Abbey acolytes.

CHAPTER 17

TENNESSEE BREW WORKS

"MR. ROBOTO"

As the latest entrepreneurs to open in the new Brewery District of Nashville's SoBro neighborhood, Tennessee Brew Works founders Christian Spears and Garr Schwartz are urban pioneers of sorts. Located near the dead end of Ewing Avenue (which Spears would like to rename "Brewing Avenue"), the brewery and taproom facility is pretty tough to find unless you know that local rocker Jack White's Third Man Records is right around the corner.

However, the location is steeped in Nashville brewing history, only a few hundred yards away from the empty field and historical marker that reminds tourists of the once-great Gerst Brewing Company that dominated the Nashville beer scene. Spears notes, "While we were under construction, some old guy came in off the street and told us that a beer named Champagne Velvet used to come from around here, but he could have been confused. We haven't been able to find any record of that." Most likely, the man's memory was indeed a little clouded since CV was an Indiana beer brand that was brewed in Terre Haute— ironically, at the Evansville Brewing Company that was responsible for the first rerelease of Gerst Beer in the '80s. It's a nice story nonetheless…

In this slightly seedy area of downtown, Spears and Schwartz have constructed a modern forward-thinking brewery the likes of which has never been seen in Nashville since the days of Gerst. The story of the two brewer/businessmen's path to their destiny is a remarkable journey as well.

Schwartz grew up in Middle Tennessee, while Spears is a native of Annapolis, Maryland. Their parallel paths carried them through the world of high finance, where they developed a business relationship that led to a friendship and ultimately into a combination of both. Spears's discovery of craft beer sounds like a pretty typical story. He says, "It's a cliché, but after college I went on a two-month backpacking tour of Europe and realized that there was so much more to beer than the cheap stuff I drank in school."

On his 1992 sojourn, Spears tried his first pints of Guinness and English bitters. A side trip to Germany introduced him to unfiltered weiss beers. He remembers, "My favorite beer of the trip was a Franziskaner's Hefe-Weisse Dunkel, which really opened my eyes to what a beer could be. I still have the bottle cap from that one." Spears also realized that the beer never tasted as good as it did close to the source and developed a philosophy that beer needs to be consumed near where it was produced. Still, he didn't recognize that he could actually make his own beer.

Spears moved to New York City in 1993 to work for Lehman Brothers, where he eventually met a kindred soul in Garr Schwartz. During his time in Manhattan, Spears discovered he had access to all sorts of international beer styles but recognized that he was living in the tail end of the city's brewpub revolution. "All sorts of folks wanted to open a restaurant with beer without realizing that you have to commit to making both great food and great beer. Only the great ones survived," he recalls. Spears vowed not to make that sort of mistake if he ever got into the brewing business.

Christian invited Garr to a crab feast in his native state of Maryland in 2006, and as a polite southern guest, Schwartz brought some of his homebrew along. Spears tried his friend's oatmeal porter and was blown away. "I never realized that a homebrew could be so remarkable," he says. The pair started brewing together whenever they happened to be in the same town.

Spears spent some time working in London that offered more opportunities to visit brewing meccas like Ireland and Prague to discover more styles of beer to experiment with. Another business move took him to Charlotte, North Carolina, where a trip to visit his buddy in Nashville turned into a life-changing event for Spears, and coincidentally, many other Nashvillians.

Christian and Garr brewed several batches together in late April 2010. Schwartz describes his style: "I like to brew beers that I like to drink, but also that my wife won't mind trying." Others must have agreed with Schwartz's better half, because Spears was amazed by the number of people who dropped by to see what they were up to in hopes of sampling some of Garr's brews.

Since Garr was not able to sell his beer legally, there was no way to put a price on his labors, but Christian laughs, "He could sure put people to work.

You know what they say; the three rules of brewing are 1. Sanitize, 2. Sanitize and 3. Sanitize, so he took the Mr. Miyagi/Karate Kid path to teaching them by making them clean all the equipment." When the volunteers asked Garr, "When are you going to teach me to brew?" he would respond, "I am."

Two weeks later, the big flood of 2010 hit Nashville during the weekend that the two brewing buddies were manually bottling fourteen cases of their beer. Spears saw the amazing spirit of Nashville's residents as they came together to help out their neighbors and recover from the calamitous flood. Combined with the demonstrable thirst for Garr's beers, that was enough to convince Christian to make the leap and move to Nashville to start a new brewery with his friend.

Neither Spears nor Schwartz had ever joined any local homebrewing clubs because they were too busy with work and family to spend the extra time on group activities. Unconsciously, they were also avoiding outside influences while they developed their own brewing styles. Garr created a monster of a homebrewing system capable of brewing twenty-gallon batches using two turkey fryer burners, a ten-gallon mash tun and a ten-gallon hot liquor tank. Carboys were used for fermentation, and brewing twice a day could produce up to eighteen gallons of beer.

A precipitating event occurred in August 2010 when Schwartz officially snagged the Internet domain names for Tennessee Brew Works. "I thought it would be a great name, so I did it," recalls Spears. Schwartz was more dubious, saying, "I didn't want to ruin a perfectly good hobby."

If they were going to ramp up their efforts further, the two potential partners needed to discuss the ramifications with their respective families, so during the spring of 2011, both men had serious sit-downs with their loved ones. Spears admits, "Our talks were probably not totally descriptive of the future experiences, but it was our best guess." With the blessings of their families, Spears and Schwartz moved forward.

On June 15, 2011, the two partners opened up Tennessee Brew Works' first business checking account, priming the pump with their own money. Spears recalls, "We had just enough capital between us to get started at the process of possibly going broke." Seizing on their years of accumulated business acumen, the two men set up their entity and began formally investigating the intellectual property issues that might arise over the names of their proposed products.

In a creative town like Nashville that is home to major publishers and music licensing services, intellectual property is not a topic to overlook. Spears explains, "The main thing that breweries get into fights with each other

The tap handles at Tennessee Brew Works pay homage to the musicians and songwriters that made Nashville famous.

over is naming rights to beers. We wanted to posture ourselves defensively." The choice of the name Tennessee Brew Works was a very conscious one, emphasizing the importance of regional breweries that the brewers believe passionately in while at the same time inviting the entire state to claim TBW for their own.

They also consciously avoided locker room humor and overly punny names when naming their beers, instead preferring to pay homage to Nashville's and Tennessee's musical heritage. Tap handles are shaped like guitar headstocks, and their offerings of beers are known as Tennessee Sessions, referring to both sessionable beers and Nashville music recording sessions.

Arguably the most difficult part of starting up the brewery was the real estate search. Spears believed, "You can't make a bad first decision and hope to survive. But Nashville is a big city with a small town atmosphere. Once the word got out that we were looking for a location, you could tell that they knew we were coming when it was time to make an offer. We considered thirty to forty different spaces and had two handshake deals go south on us before we settled on our final spot."

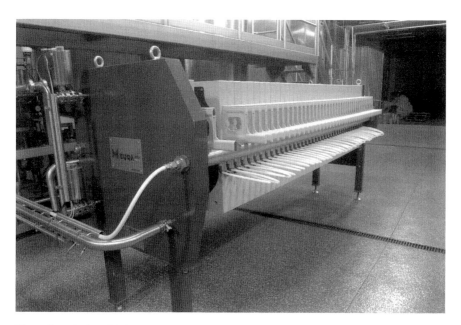

Normally only found in huge production breweries, the Meura mash filtration system at
Tennessee Brew Works was the smallest installation of its type at the time the brewery opened.

Garr Schwartz demonstrates how finely the brewery can grind its grains, thanks to the
innovative Meura Micro.

Luckily, the duo had better success raising capital for their venture and had their funding in place before they closed on the building. A last-minute deal to spin off the real estate and lease it back from one of their partners helped to move the whole process along.

The building that they settled on was a former warehouse for a printer and was only especially suitable as a brewery because it had relatively high ceilings. The partnership had to replace the electrical system, plumbing, roof and siding, taking care to save and reuse whatever material they could salvage along the way. The metal siding that lines the walls of the new taproom was once the roof of the original building. Having seen its successful work at Fat Bottom, Spears and Schwartz turned to Powell Design Studio to design the look of the new facility.

When it came time to design and procure the brewing system, the Tennessee Brew Works team members knew that they would need professional help. They discovered the team of designers and engineers from Centec to help them configure their state-of-the-art system. Since Schwartz's brewing style could be described as a Belgian/American hybrid, it was logical for Tennessee Brew Works to install a system that emphasized Belgian brewing methods.

Unlike 99 percent of American craft breweries that use the German lauter tun system to separate the liquid wort from the residual grain during the brewing process, in Belgium, 90 percent of the brewing systems employ a Meura mash filtration (MMF) system to remove the grain from the kettle. Tennessee Brew Works became the beta tester for the smallest North American installation of an MMF system, which is more popular in huge production breweries.

The MMF allows the brewery to use finely milled grain for better flavor extraction than traditional grist, so Tennessee Brew Works grinds its own wheat, barley and rye to almost a powder. The spent grain is much easier to remove since the filters capture it, dry it and compress it into cakes, which are then fed to pigs, chickens, turkeys and dairy cows at West Wind Farms.

Using the MMF system in combination with a twenty-five-barrel brewhouse from Aegir Brewing Systems results in a much more efficient brewing process, employing 50 percent less water, 20 percent less raw materials and 20 percent less electricity than conventional brewing. The system is also highly automated, with the recipes stored in a computer, allowing Schwartz to monitor and adjust the brew from a mobile phone, even remotely. This proved problematic one day when Spears thought he was alone in the brewery until Schwartz started up the grain mill from home so he could be ready to mash in when he arrived at the brewery. It took some convincing for the startled Spears not to believe that there was a ghost in the machine.

The twenty-five-barrel (technically thirty-hectolitre since it's European) system is paired with five fifty-one-barrel fermentation tanks to create six thousand barrels per year of capacity. However, the efficient brewhouse could probably handle almost ten times that much, and more tanks are a big part of future expansion plans. The entire system is hard-piped together, so instead of having to hook and unhook hoses to transfer liquid from tank to tank, one person can handle the entire brewing process and even overlap brews of different beers between batches within the same system. One brewer and one helper can complete three full brews in twelve hours from the point of mashing in.

The closed system also allows the use of a Clean in Place (CIP) system that speeds up the sanitization of the tanks between batches without having to actually get inside the huge vessels. One downside of the closed system is that Schwartz and Spears are very leery of undertaking any sour beer experiments since wild yeast could infect the entire system instead of staying intentionally isolated within one specific tank.

Since the beer is never exposed to air during the brewing process, Tennessee Brew Works can naturally condition its beers without the use of bright tanks. Unpasteurized, unfiltered and naturally conditioned like the finest champagnes, Spears and Schwartz believe their beers have superior mouth feel to traditional carbonation methods.

Schwartz had compiled fifteen recipes from his homebrewing days that he felt were appropriate for scaling up for production brewing, but out of the gate, he and Spears limited the list to five core brews. The scalability of the brewing system is another huge advantage, so Tennessee Brew Works doesn't employ pilot brewing for experimental or small batches.

The new brewery's first product was named Opening Act and was released on September 6, 2013, the same day as Black Abbey's Jude. Opening Act was an American blonde ale that was easy to drink and a fine introduction to the TBW portfolio. By the middle of the next month, all five of the Tennessee Sessions original flagship beers were brewed and in the market.

Extra Easy is Tennessee Brew Works' name for its malt-forward English pale ale/ESB hybrid made with Millennium, Goldings and Centennial hops. At 5.25 percent ABV, Extra Easy is one of TBW's most sessionable beers. Also easy to enjoy in multiples is Southern Wit, a 5.14 percent ABV wheat and pilsner malt beer with nice citrus notes.

Basil Ryeman is Tennessee Brew Works' nod to Nashville's historic Ryman Auditorium, known as the "Mother Church of Country Music."

The brewhouse at Tennessee Brew Works is hard-piped and highly automated to create an extremely efficient brewing system.

The farmhouse ale/saison benefits from the spicy nature of the rye to create a very food-friendly brew. Knowing that they couldn't open without a good IPA, Spears and Schwartz created Cutaway IPA, a citrusy example of a typical India Pale Ale made with five different varieties of hops.

The fifth and final core beer is Country Roads, a sweet potato stout made with yams sourced from a local farmer and roasted for Tennessee Brew Works by a neighboring catering company. Each batch requires cooking 240 pounds of sweet potatoes to mix into the mash. "We had to ask the Belgians if it would work," relates Schwartz. "They told us to go ahead and try it, so we did."

In addition to the five Tennessee Sessions, Tennessee Brew Works offers one seasonal beer at a time including a Rosemary Pale Ale for autumn, a 100 percent wheat beer with lime zest called Walk the Lime during the spring and a summer Farmer's Beet farmhouse ale.

Other specials occasionally make their way on to the taps at Tennessee Brew Works, and high-gravity beers are definitely in the brewery's sights for the future. In fact, it was a Belgian Trippel that Schwartz and Spears were bottling that fateful flood weekend, and they look forward to releasing that same recipe as soon as they receive their distillery license.

The sleek taproom at Tennessee Brew Works offers a bird's-eye view of the patio from the upper deck.

The final step in the journey of Tennessee Brew Works was the opening of the massive taproom. After a soft opening on Halloween, Tennessee Brew Works officially invited the public into its home on December 13, 2013, fearless of the fact that it was Friday the 13th.

The taproom is massive at 3,600 square feet, with two separate bars, growler filling stations, an outdoor patio facing (Br)Ewing Avenue and an upper deck above the street. The interior is separated into several different drinking areas with multiple locations for live musicians to perform and intentionally narrow communal tables for beer lovers to meet new friends and enjoy pints of beer. Prime spots have full views of the modern brewing equipment so that patrons can really see where their beer comes from.

Christian and Garr hope to add a full kitchen someday to prepare food for their guests and process ingredients for their exotic beers, but for now they depend on visiting food trucks and caterers to feed the masses.

In addition to taproom sales and growler fills, Tennessee Brew Works beers are currently available in more than 125 outlets ranging from Clarksville to Chattanooga. Even though it started distributing its wares later than the original plan, Tennessee Brew Works is already ahead of pace compared to its initial estimates. When it does begin to bring back some of its high-grav recipes from Garr's portfolio, it has already installed a separate system for growler fills to satisfy Tennessee's regulations regarding high-alcohol sales.

While expansion is definitely part of their plans, Schwartz promises that they will never commoditize their beer. He says, "We don't have the economy of scale to make cheap beer; we couldn't afford to peel all those potatoes. We're hyper focused on selling our current beers rather than just trying to add taps at new locations. We tried to avoid the dangerous problem that many craft brewers make of starting out too small. Most importantly, we want to make sure that our beers still taste like Garr's homebrews."

With plenty of room to add fermentation tanks and possibly a bottling line in its current facility, Tennessee Brew Works' future growth should take care of itself as more craft beer fans discover its products.

CHAPTER 18

LITTLE HARPETH BREWING

"RIVER OF DREAMS"

Little Harpeth Brewing is a brewery that is full of dualities. Despite the company's environmentally conscious attitude and playful outdoorsy advertising motif, the actual facility is located in a gritty industrial warehouse section just across the Cumberland River from downtown Nashville. The principals of the company are like yin and yang as well. Executive director Michael Kwas is young and outgoing, while head brewer Steve Scoville is sixty years old and would probably not often be described as gregarious. Kwas is more artistic and admits that he has no talent for detail. Scoville, on the other hand, considers himself to be binary and operates in absolutes.

Somehow, the two halves of the whole complement each other nicely in the business and get along quite well—which is fortunate considering that they are basically the only two employees. Little Harpeth hired its first part-time helper in mid-2014, but for the first three years of the brewery's inception and creation, the team of Kwas and Scoville did all of the heavy lifting.

Kwas grew up in suburban Bellevue west of Nashville and moved to Denver to work as an auditor for an accounting firm. While he was there, Kwas got the chance to look at the books of several breweries and got the idea that possibly this was an industry that he would like to get involved in.

Returning home to Nashville, Kwas found a job in the closest spot he could get to a brewery at the time, delivering kegs of Budweiser for local distributor Ajax Turner. Through this gig, in early 2011, Kwas came in contact with the Music City Brewers club and met Scoville, who had been homebrewing for more than a decade.

Just about every homebrew group has at least one character who earns the title of "the lager guy." At MCB, Scoville was that guy. Most homebrewers prefer to brew and drink ales for a variety of reasons. Hop lovers enjoy the mind-blowing hoppy style of many ales, and the top-fermenting ale yeasts are more forgiving to work with. Fermenting at higher temperatures and in a much shorter amount of time, ales are just easier to brew.

Steve Scoville is not the sort of man who likes to take the easy way out. Kwas was drawn to the elder brewer's dedication to his obsession and asked him for advice finding a brewer for his potential business venture of starting his own brewery. Scoville offered himself for the position and suggested that the two brew together on Scoville's half-barrel system to see if they were compatible.

"We dated for a half year and then went down to the State building in May of 2011 to get hitched," Scoville jokes. The two partners each took half of their new LLC and started to work on a business plan together.

"We knew it wouldn't be easy," recalls Kwas. "Ninety percent of the craft beer market is ales, and Steve was interested in these obscure German techniques. But he had proved through his homebrewing that he could make this work, and frankly it's not unusual for either of us to go counter to society."

They named their fledgling brewery Little Harpeth after the river that flowed near Kwas's home in Bellevue. "Beer is supposed to be fun and is part of so many recreational activities," explains Kwas. "Plus you need great water to make great beer." A friend designed a street sign–style logo featuring a stick figure on a rope swing over a river. Three stars in the logo represent the stars on the state flag, and the company puts its money where its mouth drinks by supporting the Harpeth River Watershed Association through river cleanup efforts with Team Green, a local outdoors club.

Neither Kwas nor Scoville is much of a hophead, preferring to emphasize malt characteristics in their brews, so German-inspired craft lagers were the perfect vehicles to share their love of grains. Scoville practices decoction mashing, as opposed to traditional infusion mashing where the mash is heated directly to go from one temperature to another. In decoction, or step mashing, a portion of the grain is boiled to extract more starch and break down the cell walls of the grains and then introduced back into the vessel to raise the temperature of the mixture. This process releases even more complex malty flavors to the final product.

When it came time to purchase a brewing system, Scoville spoke to fifteen different manufacturers about the sort of beers he wanted to make and the techniques he wanted to employ. "The two German companies understood

The "swinging man" logo of Little Harpeth Brewing showcases the company's dedication to fun outdoorsy activities.

The brewhouse system at Little Harpeth is more complex than most smaller craft breweries to allow for Steve Scoville's commitment to lagers and decoction mashing.

what I was talking about, but only two out of thirteen American companies got it," relates Scoville, though he admits that his persnickety nature might have made it a little more difficult for him to get his point across to some of the brewery engineers. In the end, JVNW was able to manufacture and deliver the food service heatable vessels and pumps that Scoville wanted.

They settled on a twenty-barrel five-vessel brewhouse with a separate cereal cooker for the decoction process and an additional lagering tank. Fermenting and conditioning take place in two sets of three twenty-barrel tanks. Little Harpeth's system is very specialized to handle complex mashing capabilities, and the company may try to partner with some of the new crop of micro distilleries opening in the area to assist with making their wash. The system is currently only the fourth lager-based microbrewery east of the Mississippi River.

Kwas and Scoville sought out $1.2 million in investment capital to finance their operation since traditional debt financing was unavailable for this sort of venture. By May 2013, they had raised enough money from friends and family and friends of friends to move forward. That same month, after looking at almost fifty potential buildings and making serious runs at three of them, Little Harpeth finally signed a ten-year lease on ten thousand square feet of a warehouse that had been constructed near the east bank of the Cumberland River in 1950.

They ordered their brewery equipment in July for a January 2014 delivery, but Scoville and Kwas aren't the sorts to twiddle their thumbs and wait around for anything. They set to work rehabilitating the space and preparing it to serve as a functioning brewery.

Scoville's background as a contractor was invaluable, and Kwas's commitment to sustainable practices required that the two of them do most of the work themselves to ensure the most ecological practices possible and also to preserve their precious capital. The duo saved everything from the demolition except for bent nails and broken sheets of drywall. Light fixtures, switches, door handles and drywall screws were salvaged for reuse in the build-out, and the old wiring that they ripped out to upgrade the electrical system actually paid back into the building fund in the form of scrap value for the copper. In the end, the entire project only filled half of a construction dumpster, much to the chagrin of the dumpster rental company, which called every week expecting to make a little more money picking up and dropping off a new waste bin.

All the while, Scoville continued brewing in his garage until he couldn't wait any longer to take advantage of the new space. He ripped the system out of his home and brought it to the construction site. They hard-piped the burners of the system to the building's natural gas supply and used an Igloo cooler as their mash tun. Not only did they produce the first official batches of Little Harpeth beer on this system, they used it to receive their Brewer's License from the Department of Agriculture. The inspector arrived expecting to see a full-scale brewery, but since it hadn't yet arrived, Scoville demonstrated his mini/micro/nanobrewery to the agency's satisfaction.

Once the JVNW system arrived in January and was installed, Little Harpeth was officially in business. Since lager brewing takes longer than ales, sometimes up to thirteen hours, and the fermentation process can take up to three times as long, they had no time to waste. Scoville does continue to develop techniques to shorten production times, but the entire process is definitely time, labor and capital intensive.

Little Harpeth made its first keg delivery off the big system on March 17, 2014. True to his roots as a homebrewer, Scoville continues to brew every batch in parallel on his pilot system and send samples to a laboratory in Lexington, Kentucky, to ensure that the large system produces product that is as similar to his small-batch recipes as possible.

The company tries to keep a focus on ecological practices, employing low-energy boil tactics, purchasing grain from Rahr Corporation that has been malted using fossil-free processes and even saving its spent grain for a local farmer to feed her pigs (in return for a pig roast some time in the future).

Little Harpeth offers five regular brews with the intention to expand its line and play with some high-gravity beers and even meads in the future. Its most interesting product is probably Chicken Scratch, an American pilsner made from malted barley, locally grown corn and *humulus lupulus neomexicanus*, the only variety of hops native to America. The corn is milled at the old Spencer Mill in Dickson, west of Nashville, and Little Harpeth's steady business with the small mill should allow it to invest in returning the facility to old-style water generation milling.

Upstream is Little Harpeth's San Francisco lager, a California Common–style amber beer with resinous notes of Northern Brewer hops. Similar in style to the famous Anchor Steam, Upstream has gained great acceptance on local taps. High Water is a dunkel lager inspired by brown beers from Munich breweries. Spicy bitterness on the nose and tongue characterize this particular beer.

Stax is a black lager that is surprisingly light considering its inky appearance. Full of roasty malt flavors and a bready backbone, Stax is made by blending two separate mash fermentations together. The final standard

Little Harpeth still uses Scoville's original pilot brewing system to brew parallel batches to compare with its large production brewhouse.

Little Harpeth's Mark Kwas enjoys a small quaff of Stax at the Nashville Predators Craft Beer Festival.

offering is a doppelbock called Double Paddle. Brewed in the Franciscan style, dopplebocks were the "liquid bread" that monks used for sustenance during times of fasting. At 10 percent ABV, you might not even remember you were hungry after a couple of these.

As of the summer of 2014, Little Harpeth was available in about thirty-five locations in Middle Tennessee. Future plans may include cobbling together a small taproom to add onto the building and take advantage of the spectacular view of the Cumberland River and downtown Nashville skyline from the back dock door of Little Harpeth's facility and the fact that it is located just a short walk from LP Field, the home of the Tennessee Titans. Little Harpeth has already hosted a Brew-Grass party with live music and food trucks on its back parking lot, so as more people discover where it is and how special its beers are, the brewery should continue to grow in popularity.

PART III

OTHER BREWERY PROJECTS

Yesterday, Today and Tomorrow

CHAPTER 19

BREWING IN THE HINTERLANDS

"DARKNESS ON THE EDGE OF TOWN"

In addition to the brewpubs and production breweries that are producing ales and lagers for Nashville drinkers, there are several opportunities to encounter a new brew for beer lovers willing to drive a little bit out of town. While none of these facilities currently ship their products to Nashville bars and restaurants, they are still a part of the Middle Tennessee brewing culture.

Closest to Nashville is Granite City Food and Brewery, an outpost of a national brewpub chain based out of St. Cloud, Minnesota. With thirty-one locations, Granite City has established an unusual model that it calls "fermentus interruptus," in which it brews its wort in a central facility and ships it in tankers to individual locations for final fermentation and conditioning.

The Cool Springs location of Granite City opened in Franklin on February 1, 2013, with a full menu of food, wine, cocktails and five signature beers. Its standard offerings are dictated by corporate headquarters since the recipes have been decided by the time the wort arrives via truck, but patrons can usually expect to find at least a few specialty and seasonal brews rotating throughout the year.

Broad Axe is Granite City's version of an Irish oatmeal stout, poured with a thick head and notes of coffee and chocolate. The Bennie is the brewery's nickname for its Brother Benedict's Bock, a medium-bodied German-style brown bock lager. The Duke of Wellington IPA is a classic English India Pale Ale with big hops and strong malt characteristics. The Northern is Granite City's light American lager that is the closest thing to the megabreweries' light beer offerings that are so popular with the beer-drinking public.

Granite City Food and Brewery is a modern eatery located near Cool Springs Galleria in Franklin.

The fifth standard offering at Granite City isn't exactly a separate recipe. The Two Pull is simply a version of a Black and Tan made from a blend of Northern Light and Benedict Bock. Across the chain, there may be as many as twenty different special beers on tap at any one time, so visitors can expect something novel on the extra taps at Granite City.

Farther to the southeast of Nashville is Old Shed Brewing Company in Tullahoma, Tennessee. Founders Mike Ramsey and Mike Thornburg were neighbors who each homebrewed in their garages. After a few years of talking about it, they finally decided to open a small commercial brewery in 2012. After receiving their official licenses, the Mikes delivered their first kegs of Old Shed's flagship Southern Pale Ale to three local bars on May 19, 2012.

The initial reception was overwhelming with more than one thousand pints sold on the first night at taverns with the charming names of Fast Jack's, London's and Daddy Billy's. With almost thirty kegs sold in the first week, Mike and Mike found themselves brewing almost constantly on their tiny two-barrel system while keeping their day jobs.

The duo had always hoped to upgrade to a new brewing system in the ten-barrel range, but a trip to California to visit Premier Stainless Systems led to the purchase of a brand-new fifteen-barrel brewhouse that was delivered in mid-2013. To show off its new equipment and sell more beer, Old Shed opened its own taproom on November 16, 2013. In addition to brewery tours and growler fills, Old Shed has an outdoor beer garden where patrons can enjoy pints and comestibles from local food trucks.

Old Shed now distributes its beer from Clarksville, Tennessee, to Huntsville, Alabama, but has not cracked the Nashville market yet. In addition to its Southern Pale Ale, other popular Old Shed brews include Haystack IPA, Pot Belly Porter, Honey Do Golden, Smoke House Stout and Spicy Lemon Saison.

Clarksville has its own brewpub in the form of Blackhorse Pub and Brewery. When owner Jeff Robinson retired from a military career as a helicopter pilot at nearby Fort Campbell, he and his wife, Sherri, decided to stick around Clarksville and opened Franklin St. Pub in 1992. Three years later, they opened the Blackhorse Brewery right next door and knocked out the wall between their two ventures in 1996.

In July 2013, Blackhorse Pub and Brewery expanded to a new location in Knoxville, Tennessee, but the original spot in historic downtown Clarksville will always be home base for the Robinsons, even though Sherri grew up in Knoxville and the couple met at the University of Tennessee. After an F4 tornado struck downtown Clarksville on January 29, 1999, and ripped the second story off of Blackhorse, the Robinsons didn't hesitate to rebuild.

Blackhorse serves five regular house brews, plus there's always a seasonal on tap, and the brewers like to experiment with barrel aging on occasion. The most popular brew at Blackhorse is their Barnstormer Red Ale, crafted with Hallertau hops. Blackhorse Ale is an American light lager to serve as a gateway beer for new customers, and a Vanilla Cream Ale is also popular with craft beer neophytes. More experienced beer drinkers enjoy Blackhorse's McGee's Pale Ale and Coalminer's Stout, two beers that are more traditional and assertive in style.

CHAPTER 20

CONTRACT BREWS

"WORKIN' FOR A LIVING"

Not all the beers made by Middle Tennessee brewers are released under the brand names of their respective breweries. Contract brews are a regular part of many breweries' business models, and some of them have made major inroads in the market while helping to keep production schedules full.

Blackstone Brewing Company is one of the most active contract brewers in the area, and owner Kent Taylor has used the extra income to help expand the capacity at his production brewery. Thanks to head brewer Dave Miller's previous relationship with Schlafly Beer during his three years working there in St. Louis, Blackstone entered into a contract to produce Schlafly's Pale Ale in kegs.

The alliance was logical for more reasons than just Miller's experience as the head brewer at Schlafly's taproom in St. Louis. Both Blackstone and Schlafly employ thirty-barrel brewhouses and fermenters of the same design, so quality assurance is much easier to ensure when the two companies work together. Sharing the belief that beer is better closer to the point of manufacture, Schlafly and Blackstone can better provide fresher beer to Schlafly fans and customers in the region around Nashville from Blackstone's brewing facility.

Blackstone also brews for the revitalized Falls City brands of beer. The popular Louisville-based brewery originally opened in 1905, but the Kentucky facility closed in 1978. A group of investors purchased the brands in the late 1990s and contracted the brewing out to the Pittsburgh Brewing

Blackstone carves out room on the production brewery floor for a massive wall of Schlafly kegs.

Company for several years. In 2010, the brand was revitalized with brewing functions farmed out to Sand Creek Brewing Company in Black River Falls, Wisconsin, and later to Blackstone.

Blackstone currently brews Falls City's English Pale Ale, but there are no plans to revive the company's collectors' favorite of Billy Beer. On Fridays, Blackstone also brews the wash for Nashville-based distillery Popcorn Sutton's White Whiskey, a product made in the memory of its famous namesake, legendary East Tennessee moonshiner Marvin "Popcorn" Sutton.

When Jim and Jerry Chandler bought the Gerst Haus Restaurant from the Gerst family in 1988, they wanted to revive the old Gerst Amber Ale brand of beer. After contract brewing stints at Evansville Brewing and Pittsburgh Brewing, the Chandlers turned to Yazoo's Linus Hall in 2011 to discuss the possibility of moving production back to the original hometown of the brewery. Yazoo had recently moved into its new larger production facility and had the tank room to handle the new brew, but the Chandlers were concerned about the variation in quality from batch to batch that they had experienced with their previous contract brewers.

The Chandlers did not have the old original recipes for Gerst, but they knew what they were looking for. Yazoo brewed trial batches until the taste profile was accepted. "Even if we had the original recipes," remembers Hall, "the beer would have tasted different anyway since the characteristics of different grains have changed through the years and hop varieties come and go. We decided to add some flaked corn to an altbier recipe to give it a post-Prohibition feel. It's a good easy-drinking beer with historical significance, and we're proud of the achievement."

Nashville mayor Karl Dean tapped the first keg of the new old beer at the Gerst Haus on March 25, 2011. As he enjoyed the first pint, Dean remarked that Gerst and Yazoo represented "a link between Nashville brewing past and future." Yazoo eventually bottled Gerst in a package with a replica of the old label and sells the beer as part of its brand portfolio as part of a royalty deal with the Chandlers. It has since grown to be a good seller in all of Yazoo's distribution markets.

Another contract brew project for Yazoo is a line of private label beers for its distributor, Lipman Brands. The beer was originally called Hap & Harry's Lynchburg Lager when it was released in 2011. The name came from Hap Motlow of the family that owned Jack Daniel's Distillery in Lynchburg, Tennessee, and Harry Lipman, one of the patriarchs of the ownership family of the Middle Tennessee distribution company of Jack Daniel's products.

When Jim and Jerry Chandler moved the production of Gerst Beer back to Nashville with Yazoo Brewing Company, they revived the old Gerst script "G" and dove logo for the label. *Courtesy of Scott Mertie.*

Hap used to tell Harry, "To make great whiskey, you gotta make great beer." So it was a logical extension to link the two families in a beer. Lipman also distributes Yazoo, so it asked its partner to brew a series of easy-drinking products for fans of both Tennessee whiskey and beer. Eventually changing the name to recognize the entire state, Hap and Harry's Original Tennessee Ale and Tennessee Lager are 5.4 percent ABV beers that Yazoo brews as part of its regular rotation.

It's not just large companies that take advantage of contract brewing, though. In 2008, Mark Dunkerly was working in sports marketing and fundraising at Arizona State University in Tempe. A buddy from grad school approached him with the idea of moving to Richmond, Virginia, to start a brewery. Both of them definitely saw the opportunity to ride the wave of the growing craft beer scene, but there was the small problem that neither potential partner had any brewing experience.

Undaunted, Dunkerly figured that since he was thirty-one years old and single with no kids, it was as good a time as any to make the leap and signed on to handle sales and marketing for the new venture. He planned a two-month barbecue odyssey from August to September for him to try some of the greatest smoked meats in the country as he made his way across the United States to his new home. Unfortunately, by the time he arrived in Richmond in October 2008, the stock market had crashed and the financing for the new brewery fell through.

However, along the way, Dunkerly had stopped in Louisville, Kentucky, to visit Bluegrass Brewing Company (BBC). While there, he discussed the prospect of contract brewing with them. He learned about a project called Horse Piss Beer that BBC brewed on contract. A portion of the proceeds from the brand went to benefit a local charity for disabled jockeys. Although the name of the beer turned Dunkerly off a little bit, the charitable business model fascinated him.

He decided to leave Richmond and return to his hometown of Nashville in the summer of 2009 to try to replicate the charitable model. He figured he would get a day job in marketing and sell beer on the side. Ultimately, he ended up reversing the order of the process.

Another former classmate friend of Dunkerly's was working at a Nashville nonprofit called the Oasis Center. Dunkerly was impressed by the organization's mission to "provide at-risk youth a connection to a caring adult, a safe & secure environment, and empowerment to make better choices" and was blown away by its facilities and work after a visit.

With BBC in place as a contract brewer and Oasis selected as the beneficiary of the charitable donations, all Dunkerly had to do was select a beer and figure out a name for it. A Google search of "Nashville" resulted in the story of Fisk's Jubilee Singers, an African American a capella group that has been spreading goodwill around the world and drawing attention to the city for almost 150 years. The dictionary defines the word "jubilee" as "a festive celebration, a gathering of friends." All of these connotations sounded exactly like what Dunkerly was hoping to promote with his new product, Jubilee Beer.

He chose a brown ale as the style for his first beer because there weren't a lot of those already in the Middle Tennessee market, and brown ales are a good gateway drink to convert new craft beer lovers. Dunkerly worked with the brewers at BBC to develop a flavor profile that emphasized sweetness with a little bit of complexity.

The first release of Jubilee Nut Brown Ale was released in bottles only in March 2010. The initial reception was very positive, but Dunkerly admits that a bottles-only release is not exactly the easiest way to build a new brand. "Consumers will pay $6.00 for a pint of craft beer on tap, but it's hard to

Jubilee's Mark Dunkerly (center) as his alter ego Randy at the Hot Chicken and Jorts event at Mayday Brewery.

convince them to spend $8.99 for a six-pack of a new beer." Unfortunately, since the beer was being brewed in Kentucky, the cost of shipping kegs to Nashville bars and returning them to the brewery when empty was prohibitive for the start-up company.

Lipman took on the distribution of Jubilee, but Dunkerly was responsible for most of the sales to the initial thirty-plus restaurants and bars that took on the brand by sitting down with the owners and telling them the story. A small number of independent grocery stores also signed up with Jubilee to sell the beer to consumers.

By 2011, Dunkerly was experiencing supply problems with Bluegrass Brewing Company as its growth made it difficult to carve out time in its production schedule for Jubilee. Dunkerly began to search for a local brewer to take over the brewing and help him develop a new product.

The answer came in the form of Ozzy Nelson at Mayday in Murfreesboro. After meeting at a tasting event, Dunkerly and Nelson developed Randy's IPA in test batches in Ozzy's backyard. Since Nelson was still crafting the business plan for his new brewery, including Jubilee in his production projections was a win/win for the brand and the brewery.

Randy's IPA is named for Dunkerly's humorous alter ego, a jean shorts–wearing, mulleted good ole boy persona that Mark dresses as at charitable events. Randy's beer is much more complex than Randy's brain, with four different malts and three varieties of hops creating a full-bodied IPA. The beer has become popular enough that Mayday brews a thirty-barrel batch of Randy's IPA every two or three weeks.

Along the way to becoming a beer baron, Dunkerly ended up actually taking a full-time job at the Oasis Center as a fundraiser. Since he spends his free time selling his beer that actually serves as an additional source of funds for the charity, Oasis ended up with the equivalent of one and a half employees in the form of Dunkerly. Everyone he comes in contact with in both his day gig and his job selling beer learns about Mark's passion for Oasis and its good works.

"People ask me why I would want to give away half my profits to a nonprofit," he says. "It's because I really believe in them, and truth be told, I know the business has been more than twice as successful than it would have been without the charitable component." Twice a year, Dunkerly distributes Oasis Center's share of the profits, a number that has contributed thousands of dollars to its coffers.

Currently, Jubilee Nut Brown Ale is on hiatus, but Dunkerly hopes to move production to Mayday some time soon. Randy's IPA is available in kegs only for growler fills and restaurants and bars, but he hopes to release it in cans eventually. The best part about packaging is that he'll have room to share the mission of Oasis on the can, and telling that story is what really moves Mark Dunkerly.

CHAPTER 21

BREWERIES THAT DIDN'T MAKE IT

"ANOTHER ONE BITES THE DUST"

Considering the average failure rate of most food service businesses, it's actually pretty amazing that all fourteen of the breweries opened in Middle Tennessee since 1994 are still operating. Only Bohannon Brewing Company didn't survive long past the turn of the century, but there have been a few failed ventures that are worth noting.

In 1994, Jack Daniel's Distillery announced plans to open a brewery at its facility in Lynchburg, Tennessee. Hoping to cash in on the mid-90s craft beer boom and trading on its worldwide brand name and experience brewing mash for its Tennessee whiskey, the distillery began test marketing Jack Daniel's 1866 Classic Amber Lager in the Nashville market in late 1994. The beer was named after the year that the distillery was officially registered by Mr. Jack himself.

The head brewer was John Barrett, who oversaw a small brewing facility that had an annual capacity of 2,400 barrels per year, but at least some of the beer was actually produced by Evansville Brewing Co. and the Hudepohl/Schoenling Brewery in Cincinnati. At the brand's peak, Jack Daniel offered seven products: Amber Lager, Oak-Aged American Ale, Oak-Aged Honey Brown Ale, Oak-Aged Pale Ale, Oak-Aged Pilsner, Oak-Aged Summer Brew and Oak-Aged Winter Brew.

Barrel-aged beers were a natural point of emphasis for Jack Daniel's, and craft breweries still use the distillery's old barrels to add complexity to modern brews. However, the Lynchburg experiment was short-lived after experimental test market expansions to Richmond, Virginia, and Baltimore,

Despite the 1866 on the label, these are not 150-year-old beer bottles. They are examples of Jack Daniel's short stint as a brewer during the 1990s. *Courtesy of Jack Daniel's Distillery.*

Maryland, were not successful enough to sustain the brand. The brewery closed at the end of 1997, although beer memorabilia collectors can still be found online gushing (incorrectly) that they have discovered a rare beer bottle that they think is almost 150 years old. Bless their hearts.

In 2009, Fred Minderman of Arrington Vineyards partnered with brewmaster Fred Scheer from Boscos in a venture they called Battle Ground Brewery. Their plan was to open a small brewpub in the old city jail in downtown Franklin, and for a year and a half, the pub part of that proposal worked out. The business operated as a restaurant and bar with live music from December 6, 2009, until May 28, 2011.

Battle Ground got as far as actually purchasing a seven-barrel brewing system from Premier Stainless, but efforts to purchase two adjoining historic buildings to house the brewery were unsuccessful as zoning regulations would not allow for the commercial operation in those spaces.

The equipment remained in mothballs while Battle Ground Brewery contracted with Atlanta's Sweetwater Brewery to brew private labels under the Battle Ground name to serve in its taproom. These brands included American Pale Ale, Light, India Pale Ale and a Brown Ale. Seasonal selections included a porter and blueberry wheat. When the brewery plans were scuttled, the entire venture was abandoned in May 2011.

Also in 2011, longtime homebrewer Mike Causey announced plans to open Broadcast Brewing Company, named after his previous career working for a media production company. Along with his brewing partner Phillip Ratliff, Causey contracted for space in the same old Fluffo mattress factory where Fat Bottom eventually built its brewery.

In preparation for ramping up to commercial brewing, Broadcast Brewing began to showcase its lines of balanced, easy-drinking beers at several festivals around Nashville. It even named one of its brews, a sweet stout, Fluffo in honor of its proposed future home. Other beers from Broadcast that hinted of its future potential included an extra pale ale and a honey ale.

Ultimately, the venture fell through before any commercial brewing equipment was ordered, and the space at the Fluffo building was filled by other businesses, most notably an excellent growler fill store called the Filling Station. So while there is only one brewery in the Main Street location today, there is still plenty of great craft beer flowing out of that building.

CHAPTER 22
FUTURE MIDDLE TENNESSEE BREWERY PROJECTS

"SHAPES OF THINGS"

One thing that most brewery owners in Middle Tennessee agree on is that there is still plenty of room for more local growth in the craft beer market. Fat Bottom's Ben Bredesen expressed this sentiment nicely on his blog: "I really believe that the more craft breweries there are in Nashville, the better we will all do." While the draft market is starting to get competitive for tap space, the potential for local bottled and canned products is only limited by the amount of shelf space at beer stores and the thirst of consumers.

Yazoo, Jackalope and Cool Springs have already entered the packaging game, and several other players are making plans to distribute their products in forms other than just draft beer. Seizing on this opportunity, Mark Kamp of Turtle Anarchy and Jason McMurray have formed an entity called Southern Anarchy Alchemy to provide all sorts of adjunct services to existing and future Middle Tennessee brewers and breweries.

Southern Anarchy plans to operate out of twenty-five thousand square feet of the old Dixie Wire building in West Nashville. In addition to housing the new thirty-barrel brewhouse for Kamp's Turtle Anarchy, Southern Anarchy will offer services like keg leasing and cleaning services, a bottling line and a canning line so that smaller breweries will be able to get into the packaging business without the expense of setting up their own systems.

Mobile packaging lines do exist, but the hassle of transporting and setting up the complicated machinery makes some brewery owners nervous. Southern Anarchy's model will allow for breweries to ship their beer in tankers to be packaged and then delivered to the distributors, and some storage capabilities may also be offered.

It looks like Scott Swygert will be the next homebrewer to make the jump into commercial brewing with his Honky Tonk Brewing Company in the Metro Center industrial development north of downtown Nashville. The brewery will be located in half of a cavernous building that locals of a certain age may remember as a dance club/pick-up bar from the '80s and '90s that was called the Heartthrob Café. (Then again, maybe they may not remember it…it was that kind of place.)

As of August 2014, Honky Tonk was still under construction as Swygert has been doing most of the work himself. Formerly in real estate ventures, Swygert recognized the value of the building that had remained vacant for years. Thanks to high ceilings and a completely open floor plan, Swygert was able to lay out the taproom and brewery space to his own specifications. Since the office park empties after 5:00 p.m., there should be plenty of parking for visitors to the future fifty-seat taproom during the limited hours that it will be open.

Swygert has pieced together a brew system by scouring equipment from all over the world, including old dairy tanks and a vessel from Italy. The system will have a direct-fired twenty-five-barrel brewhouse that he has insulated and covered with diamond plating that looks like the running boards of a tricked-out pickup truck. Figuring that steel piping doesn't cost that much more than hoses, Swygert has hard-piped the entire system that should increase the efficiency of the brewing process and simplify cleanup between batches.

Other novel additions are a plastic cold liquor tank that will be housed in the walk-in keg storage room to facilitate cooling. Swygert seized the opportunity to purchase a huge one-hundred-barrel bright tank from Sweetwater at a price per gallon that is much cheaper than he would have paid for smaller tanks.

Swygert plans to begin brewing at Honky Tonk sometime in the second half of 2014 and will self-distribute within Davidson County. He may also use his fifteen-gallon homebrewing rig for specials, but his main offering will be four year-round brews plus seasonals.

Another new brewery project was announced in June 2014 with Smith and Lentz Brewing signing a lease on yet another space in Nashville's Brewery District. Although opening dates and details of the brewery are still up in the air, on April 23, 2014, Kurt Smith and Adler Lentz applied to sell beer both on and off premise at their future location at 537 Fifth Avenue

Scott Swygert on the brewing deck of his new venture, Honky Tonk Brewing Company.

South, which should put them less than a one-hundred-yard stagger around the corner from Czann's.

Other announced future projects include French Landing Brewing Company, an ambitious brewery/restaurant facility planned for 1612 Church Street in Nashville's Midtown neighborhood. The brewery is named after a variation of one of Nashville's first names given to the wilderness settlement by Timothy Demonbreun, a French fur trapper who was one of the area's first settlers. French Landing is the brainchild of Eric Janson, and quite a brain it is. Janson earned his PhD in biological sciences from Vanderbilt University. After completing an apprenticeship at Jackalope, Dr. Janson left his comfortable postgraduate research job in 2012 to pursue his dream of opening a brewery.

Plans are to brew five regular recipes year round with seasonal specialties mixed in to French Landing's offerings. Janson's preference is for American-style craft beers, but he doesn't dismiss the possibility of experimenting with more exotic styles and barrel-aged products. Initially expecting to distribute draft beer only in the brewery/restaurant and to other local establishments, French Landing does hope to move into consumer packaging in the future.

Tail Gate Beer is an already established brewery out of San Diego that was founded in 2007 by Wesley Keegan. In June 2014, Keegan announced that he would be moving his operation to West Nashville at 7600 Charlotte Pike, the former home of a Loyal Order of Moose Lodge. Plans include converting the lodge's old baseball field into an outdoor amphitheater for acoustic music along with picnic, tailgate and event spaces. Tail Gate also hopes to grow hops on the property to use in its products.

Tail Gate specializes in small-batch experimental beers distributed in cans and hopes to expand its selection of inventive recipes after the move to Music City. Past releases include coffee and chocolate stouts, pumpkin ales and an American pale ale flavored with grapefruit. Keegan is committed to hiring a local brewmaster once the facility is operational and expects his new brewer to continue to push the envelope in the brewery's small tanks and multiple fermenters. Future visitors will be able to enjoy Tail Gate Beer in the brewery's taproom or in cans distributed across the state.

In August 2014, Paul Vaughn and Kavon Togry announced plans to open Bearded Iris Brewing Co. at 101 Van Buren Street in Germantown. The pair hopes to build out a 1,200-square-foot taproom to serve their style of Belgian and French Saison beers plus barrel-aged products. Both owners have experience as homebrewers, and Vaughn has apprenticed at commercial breweries as well. Bearded Iris hopes to begin brewing by the end of 2014 and has already begun to showcase its wares at tasting events around Nashville.

CHAPTER 23

SERVICE PROVIDERS AND ASSOCIATED GROUPS

"YOU'VE GOT A FRIEND"

While the entrepreneurs who have built their own breweries and carried Nashville's craft beer industry on their collective backs forward into the twenty-first century are all worthy of note, there are other significant contributors who have operated behind the scenes as catalysts for the region's growth as a major player.

Canned beers have made a resurgence in popularity among craft beer drinkers and brewers, but the South has lagged behind in acceptance. Cole Lanham and father-son team Mo and Carl Oelker aim to change that with their new Chattanooga and Bowling Green–based venture, Toucan Mobile Canning. Toucan is an affiliate of Mobile Canning Systems (MCS) out of Longmont, Colorado.

Toucan's affiliate agreement with MCS grants it a territory of a 150-mile radius around Chattanooga, an area with more than one hundred breweries within the footprint. Since air and light are the mortal enemies of good beer, the canning process can help protect the contents from both. Toucan's process allows it to deliver its mobile equipment to a brewery inside of a box van and then connect directly to the bright tanks.

The beer is pumped from the bright tanks through the filling heads of the canner and into the packaging. Toucan works with breweries to design and fabricate their cans, limiting the inventory of packaging that producers need to keep on hand. Easily recyclable, aluminum packaging offers environmental benefits over glass.

Another aspect of the craft beer experience is maintaining clean lines at the ultimate point of distribution. For years, bar owners and consumers alike paid little attention to the cleanliness of their tap systems, leading to all sorts of impurities adding unpleasant tastes to the commodity beer that flowed through the lines. Although some would claim that these impurities might be the most interesting flavors of typical cheap American light lagers, real craft brew aficionados recognize the difference.

Bar owners, beer distributors and breweries all contract with a Nashville firm called A Head for Profits for tap system installation and maintenance. After all the work that goes into making these craft beers, there is no sense in allowing "off" flavors to sully the brew, and A Head for Profits has grown into a company with almost twenty employees in just three years of operation.

Its well-organized multiple-tap system designs and installations also allowed craft beer bars and growler filling stores to more easily manage taking kegs on and off their systems, providing consumers with access to more options of craft beer. Before A Head for Profits, convenience dictated buying larger stores of fewer brands of beer for simplicity's sake, depriving beer lovers from the opportunity to discover new and different styles and breweries.

A Head for Profits also offers setup, teardown and event management services for beer festivals, and Nashville has more than a handful of those. Middle Tennessee beer lovers can mark their calendars for at least one major craft beer event just about any month of the year. Major opportunities to sample beers and meet the brewers include: Main Street Brew Fest in downtown Franklin, East Nashville Beer Festival, Eastside Brew Ha Ha, MAFIAoZA'S Music City Brewer's Fest, Nashville Predators Craft Beer Festival, Taste of Tennessee Craft Brewers Festival, Beer Fest in the Gulch, Nashville Beer Festival, Germantown Oktoberfest, Tennessee Beer Festival, 12 South Winter Warmer, Brew at the Zoo, Tennessee Volksfest, Yum East and the Music City Brew Fest.

The man behind many of the best festivals in town and undoubtedly one of the major contributors to the growth of craft beer in Nashville is Matt Leff of Rhizome Productions. Leff moved to Nashville from Atlanta to pursue a career in information technology. After surveying the craft beer community in his adopted hometown, he found it lacking. Rather than just complain about the few festivals in town that tended to be more like drunk fests with patrons swilling national brands of light lagers, Leff decided to do something about it and organized the first East Nashville Beer Festival (ENBF) in 2011.

Leff intentionally limits the number of tickets sold for the festivals he plans so that attendees and exhibitors will have the time and space to actually interact and talk about the beers that are being poured. Leff attracted

Crowds enjoying samples at the Nashville Predators Beer Festival at the Bridgestone Arena, home to the Predators NHL hockey club.

regional craft beer players from around the region to the first ENBF, and local brewers took notice of the interest of the crowd that attended the event in East Park.

The successful first festival led to Leff forming Rhizome Productions to serve as the organizing company behind festivals in Nashville, Dallas, Tupelo, Chattanooga and Greenville, South Carolina. He insists that every one of his festivals have a charitable component and has contributed more than $200,000 from the proceeds of his festivals to local organizations over the first three years of Rhizome's existence.

Leff is also the major organizer of Nashville Craft Beer Week and runs a tour operation in partnership with Gray Line of Tennessee under the name of the Nashville Brew Bus to transport craft brew fans from taproom to taproom on weekend runs.

The homebrewing community of Middle Tennessee is also very strong thanks to past and present organizations like the Antioch Sud Suckers, Misfits of Brewing Science, Mid-State Brew Club, Reformed Brewers Fellowship and the Music City Brewers. The MCB is probably the largest club in the area with about one hundred active members and many more following the group on social media. In addition to formal monthly meetings, members gather informally on Wednesday nights at Boscos to share their experiences with homebrewing. At one time during the early part of this century, future master brewers Linus Hall of Yazoo, Karen Lassiter of Boscos, Carl Meier of Black Abbey, Steve Scoville of Little Harpeth and Ken Rebman of Czann's were all members of the Music City Brewers at the same time.

Many of these professional brewers have also joined together as members of the Tennessee Craft Brewers Guild, a nonprofit organization that was formed in 2011 with the mission of "promoting and protecting the great craft breweries in Tennessee." The group sponsors educational and tasting events but, even more importantly, serves as an informational vehicle to communicate with local and state government with regard to the interests of the craft brewing industry.

And Tennessee brewers certainly have had some issues for government to address over the past few years. The group came together to address the specific issue of Tennessee's abnormally high beer taxes in 2011. Thanks to an antiquated triple-layer beer tax, barrels of craft beer in the state were taxed at a rate that was 12 percent higher than any other state in the country. Instead of figuring tax rates based on volume, the state charged based on the cost of the beer, so more expensive craft beers were at a distinct disadvantage to the huge commodity breweries and their lower-cost products.

Regionally, the numbers were even more discouraging as Tennessee brewers were charged $37.00 per barrel in tax for craft beer versus $7.51 in Arkansas and $13.23 in Mississippi. The Tennessee Craft Brewers Guild organized a grass-roots campaign called "Fix the Beer Tax" that argued to the legislature that craft brewers were at an economic disadvantage, limiting expansion and future job creation. Several major regional and national craft beer breweries passed on Tennessee as an option for brewery expansion, partly due to their objection to the state's beer tax structure.

Consumers rallied behind the effort and contacted their legislators, urging them to address this inequity. In April 2013, both the State House and Senate overwhelmingly passed the Beer Tax Reform Act of 2013 that was then signed into law by Governor Bill Haslam. In the end, legislators agreed that the state must remain competitive in the fast-growing craft beer industry.

In early 2014, after years of debate, the legislature passed a controversial bill that legalized the sale of wine in grocery stores. Most Capitol Hill watchers figured that senators and representatives wouldn't have the appetite

Linus Hall signing a bottle of the Beacon, a collaborative brewing project with Calfkiller to raise funds to support efforts to fix Tennessee's beer tax. *Photo by Adam Jones, courtesy of Yazoo Brewing Company.*

to address any more alcohol regulatory issues in the session, and since the craft beer effort had received its tax concessions the previous year, that would be the last reform the industry could expect anytime soon.

But the Tennessee Craft Brewers Guild wasn't finished yet and pushed forward with an effort it named "Fix the Beer Cap." Prior to 2014, Tennessee only considered products with an Alcohol By Weight of 5 percent or below to be beer; anything higher fell under the purview of distilled spirits laws.

Beer stores were only allowed to sell beers that fell under an ABV of 6.25 percent, with anything higher exiled to liquor stores.

Brewers couldn't legally produce beers with what would be considered moderate alcohol levels for craft beer in other states without a distillery license in addition to their brewing certificate. Surrounding states' caps for low-gravity beers ranged from 8 percent ABV to no cap at all, so Tennessee brewers again saw themselves at a decided regional disadvantage.

The guild lobbied for an increase to 12 percent ABW (15 percent ABV) in its proposed Beer Cap Reform Act of 2014, but again, most folks assumed that it would take until the legislature next convened before the proposal would get serious attention. The Tennessee Craft Brewers Guild was undeterred and pressed forward arguing the non-competitive position brewers felt they were placed in.

Guild president Linus Hall of Yazoo presented his own high-gravity beer Sue as a case study of the effect of the regressive tax. He pointed out that selling Sue meant paying $1,000 per year for a distillery license, and that it would cost him another $4,000 annually for a liquor-by-the-drink permit if he wanted to sell it in his own taproom. Despite the popularity of Sue among beer judges and consumers, the difficulties associated in distribution and sales prevented it from becoming the power brand that Hall believed it deserved to be.

His argument must have been compelling, because after a frantic publicity and lobby effort that lasted less than two months, the legislature did approve a raising of the beer cap, albeit to only 8 percent ABV instead of the requested 12 percent. Still, it was unexpected progress that can certainly be attributed to the efforts of the Tennessee Craft Brewers Guild and will benefit beer drinkers across the state.

TIMELINE OF MAJOR NASHVILLE BREWERIES

William Gerst Brewing Company	1890–1954
Bohannon Brewing Company	1988–2004
Blackstone Brewing Company	1994–present
Boscos Pizza Kitchen and Brewery	1996–present
Big River/Rock Bottom	1997–present
Yazoo Brewing Company	2003–present
Calfkiller Brewing Company	2009–present
Cool Springs Brewery	2009–present
Jackalope Brewing Company	2011–present
Turtle Anarchy Brewing Company	2012–present
Fat Bottom Brewing	2012–present
Mayday Brewery	2012–present
Czann's Brewing Company	2013–present
Black Abbey Brewing Company	2013–present
Tennessee Brew Works	2013–present
Little Harpeth Brewing	2014–present

NOTABLE NASHVILLE-AREA BREWPUBS, TAPROOMS, CRAFT BEER BARS AND GROWLER FILLING LOCATIONS

12 South Taproom and Grill
2318 Twelfth Avenue South
Nashville, TN 37204
(615) 463-7552
www.12southtaproom.com

Black Abbey Brewing Company
2952 Sidco Drive
Nashville, TN 37204
(615) 755-0070
www.blackabbeybrewing.com

Black Horse Pub and Brewery
132 Franklin Street
Clarksville, TN 37040
(931) 552-3726
www.theblackhorsepub.net

Blackstone Brewing Company
1918 West End Avenue
Nashville, TN 37203
(615) 327-9969
www.blackstonebrewery.com

Boscos Hillsboro Village
1805 Twenty-first Avenue South
Nashville, TN 37212
(615) 385-0050
www.boscosbeer.com

Broadway Brewhouse Downtown
317 Broadway
Nashville, TN 37201
(615) 271-2838
www.broadwaybrewhouse.net

Broadway Brewhouse Midtown
1900 Broadway
Nashville, TN 37203
(615) 340-0089
www.broadwaybrewhouse.net

Broadway Brewhouse West
7108 Charlotte Pike
Nashville, TN 37209
(615) 356-5005
www.broadwaybrewhouse.net

Cool Springs Brewery
600A Frazier Drive #135
Franklin, TN 37067
(615) 503-9626
www.coolspringsbrewery.com

Corsair Artisan Nashville Taproom
1200 Clinton Street #110
Nashville, TN 37203
(615) 200-0320
www.corsairtaproom.com

Craft Brewed Bottle Shop and
    Tasting Room
2502 Franklin Road
Nashville, TN 37204
(615) 873-1992
www.craftbrewednashville.com

Czann's Brewing Company
505 Lea Avenue
Nashville, TN 37203
(615) 748-1399
www.czanns.com

Fat Bottom Brewing
900 Main Street
Nashville, TN
(615) 678-5895
www.fatbottombrewing.com

The Filling Station
1118 Halcyon Avenue
Nashville, TN 37204
(615) 953-2951
www.brewstogo.com

The Filling Station East
904B Main Street
Nashville, TN 37206
(615) 457-3535
www.brewstogo.com

Flying Saucer
111 Tenth Avenue South
Nashville, TN 37246
(615) 259-3039
www.beernurd.com/stores/nashville

Frugal MacDoogal
701 Division Street
Nashville, TN 37203
(615) 242-3612
www.frugalmacdoogal.com

Granite City Food & Brewery
1864 W McEwen Drive
Franklin, TN 37067
(615) 435-1949
www.gcfb.net

Hops + Crafts
319 Twelfth Avenue South
Nashville, TN 37203
(615) 678-8631
www.hopscrafts.com

The Hop Stop
2909B Gallatin Pike
Nashville, TN 37216
(615) 739-6547
www.facebook.com/TheHopStop

Left: With locations in Nashville's growing 12 South and East Nashville neighborhoods, the Filling Station offers growler fills of many local, regional and national craft beers.

Below: The Hop Stop is a cozy East Nashville craft beer bar and growler filling location that also serves gourmet hot dogs to hungry drinkers and thirsty eaters.

Jackalope Brewing
701 Eighth Avenue South
Nashville, TN 37203
(615) 873-4313
www.jackalopebrew.com

Kay Bob's Grill & Ale
1602 Twenty-first Avenue South
Nashville, TN 37212
(615) 321-4567
www.kaybobs.us

Mayday Brewery
521 Old Salem Highway
Murfreesboro, TN 37129
(615) 479-9722
www.maydaybrewery.com

Midtown Wine and Spirits
1610 Church Street
Nashville, TN 37203
(615) 327-3874
www.midtownwineandspirits.com

M.L. Rose Craft Beer and Burgers
2535 Franklin Pike
Nashville, TN 37204
(615) 712-8160
www.ml-rose.com

M.L. Rose Craft Beer and
   Burgers West
4408 Charlotte Avenue
Nashville, TN 37209
(615) 750-2920
www.ml-rose.com

Mount Juliet Beer Company
11125 Lebanon Road
Mount Juliet, TN 37122
(615) 773-2124
www.mtjulietbeerco.com

Red Dog Wine and Spirits
1031 Riverside Drive
Franklin, TN 37064
(615) 794-9866
www.reddogwineandspirits.com

Rock Bottom Restaurant & Brewery
111 Broadway
Nashville, TN 37201
(615) 251-4677
www.rockbottom.com

Tennessee Brew Works
809 Ewing Avenue
Nashville, TN 37203
(615) 200-8786
www.tnbrew.com

Turtle Anarchy Brewing
   Company
216 Noah Drive, Suite 140
Franklin, TN 37064
(615) 595-8855
www.turtleanarchy.com

Yazoo Brewing Company
910 Division Street
Nashville, TN 37203
(615) 891-4649
www.yazoobrew.com

INDEX

ABOUT THE AUTHOR

Chris Chamberlain is a food, drink, wine, spirits, travel and personal interest writer based in Nashville, Tennessee, where he has lived his entire life except for four years in California, where he studied liberal arts at Stanford University and learned how to manipulate chopsticks. While in college, he was convinced that he could taste the difference between the Schmidt's beers that came in the cardboard twelve-pack holder with the fish on the box versus the one with the duck on it. Fortunately, he also discovered that beer could actually taste like  something thanks to his exposure to the Anchor Steam Beer brewed by a fellow Stanford alum, Fritz Maytag. Frequent visits to the Anchor Brewery were simultaneously eye-opening and eye-closing thanks to long stints in the tasting room.

He is a regular writer for the *Nashville Scene* and its "Bites" food blog as well as *Nashville Lifestyles* magazine. He is the southern correspondent for FoodRepublic.com and has also contributed to the *Nashville City Paper*, *Her Nashville*, *Relish*, *Julep*, *Local Palate*, the *Bourbon Review*, *2001 Edgehill*, the Southern Foodways Alliance's *Gravy* newsletter and as a kitchen gadget reviewer at www.geardiary.com. He has written two travel guides and cookbooks for Thomas Nelson Publishing, *The Southern Foodie: 100 Places to Eat Before You Die and the Recipes That Made Them Famous* and its sequel, *The Southern Foodie's Guide to the Pig.*

Chamberlain has attended and reported from Tales of the Cocktail in New Orleans for many years and has wide-ranging knowledge of and reviewing experience within the cocktail culture and the beer, spirits and wine industry.

In 2012, Chamberlain undertook a year-long study of barbecue for Food Republic, including profiles of notable pitmasters and their unique regional styles, judging at several competitive barbecue competitions and being embedded as a member of cook teams at the Memphis in May World Championship Barbecue Cooking Contest and the Big Apple BBQ Block Party. He has also served as a culinary judge at over a dozen different competitions across the country, including the Jack Daniel's World BBQ Championships, World Food Championships, Atlanta Wine and Food Festival Cast Iron Cookoff and the National Cornbread Cookoff. He has appeared on several national television shows including *Eat St.*; *Diners, Drive-ins and Dives*; *Unique Eats*; *Chow Masters*; *In the Kitchen with David*; *10! Show Philly*; and *More at Midday.*

One of his favorite things in life to do is to put a shoulder on the smoker and watch SEC football all day long while working his way through a growler of craft beer and waiting for his pork to reach "pig-picking" temperature as slowly as possible.